MW01616723

WAR OF ATTRITION

(SECOND EDITION)

———

Greg Walsh

Copyright © 2019 by Greg Walsh

All rights reserved.

War of Attrition is non-fiction, recollection, and observation. Events, locations, and conversations were diligently recreated from contemporaneous note and memory. In order to maintain anonymity I have changed or omitted the names of certain individuals and places. I have also changed identifying characteristics and details relating to appearance, occupation, or location when I felt it necessary.

Illustrations © 2019 by Paul Waggener and Michael Childers
Book design and pre-production by Dawn Landers
Cover design and inside photography by The Mephisto Group

ISBN: 978-0-9915771-3-2

Also by Greg Walsh

Warofattrition.com
(Stories, oddities, and observations...)

Wolfbrigade.com
(Subversive physical culture and unorthodox philosophy)

Theft of the Age (Novel)

Subversionist (Podcast)

For the subversionists,
dissenters,
unconventionalists,
naysayers,
and thought criminals.

- Resto Verus -

PMA / FFF / FTW

Table of Contents

DOOMED

With the misdirection society is plunging in, do we have even a *shot* at living simple, upstanding, moral lives?

Definition and interpretation of morality is largely subjective, however I would say that disparaging someone after, or making light of, their untimely death is flatly *immoral*.

I recently overheard a man talking about his ex-wife. He was speaking to a few women, one in particular, and casually mentioned that his wife had gotten cancer and died during the finalization of their divorce, "...*making the process easy for him*!" No remorse in his voice, no follow-up statement to make himself sound less arrogant or heartless. Instead, his crude follow up was, "*I didn't do it! I didn't do it!*"

The ladies tittered nervously, and left abruptly; I was left simply wanting to beat him. I wanted to physically punish him for the mental harm that he had just done to me and the others that heard him talking unsympathetically about the death of a woman he at one time loved enough to marry. I wanted him to look at me, dizzy and choking on blood and teeth, and understand that while punishment comes in many forms, the most primal one had just caught up with him.

I had to take a few breaths of reason to not do so, and even then, my feet were exiting the situation while my head was still right in the thick of it.

I have no doubt that his callousness will someday be punished with loneliness, failing health without sympathy, and eventually exile to the fires of hell, but none of that fucking matters. He'll never see himself for what he is: Common. The rule, not the exception; The sort of human fire alarm that should send people running either away as fast as they can, or towards at full gait to help.

But neither will happen.

People just take it, overlook it, and move along... Right into the next exploitative "reality" show or pandering, enabling talk show that flaunts human suffering, degradation, and decline JUST enough to elicit some armchair sympathy, but not quite enough to convey to the masses that the erosion of human decency and ethics are the rule now, not the exception.

What chance do we have... unless we choose to push even harder, in the opposite direction? Society is flawed mob mentality; There is no semblance of unity unless all else has failed and they have to rely on SOMEONE out of fear for their own well-being.

I don't relate to or align with any political party for many of the same reasons. They're all so caught up in rallying mindless herds around an agenda engineered for the sole purpose of making the masses feel better about how fucked up everything is, and getting them to pledge momentary loyalty to the person feeding them the false security.

They fake sincerity towards hard issues that don't really hit their homes, and then sell them, kit and caboodle, to a society that can't see past the tip of their noses unless their quality of life is being interrupted.

...And such breeds the hordes of gutless, spineless, thoughtless, and conscienceless drones that reaffirm daily that we're destined to sink deeper and deeper into society's open sewer.

No one cares... And those few that truly do, walk a path of pain.

Caring is a curse in this doomed world, and can alienate and sadden those afflicted to the point of dysfunction, with no relief other than the occasional brush with eyes that show the same struggles as their own.

BEEP-BEEP

I was riding my bicycle down a city street in Rochester, NY when some idiot and his girlfriend in a gigantic Jeep tried to veer me into the cars parked alongside us. It was a perfect east coast spring day- cool and sunny. I had a sweatshirt on, and it must have made me look a bit younger than I actually was; Bullies usually only mess with easy targets.

I avoided hitting the cars, not for the lack him trying, and as what I thought to be a passive retort, I rode in the center of the street making it briefly impossible for him to pass by. I was confused and pissed, but intent on enjoying the day... I was on my way to a friends' house, so I opted to inconvenience him for just a minute and then turn off towards my destination.

The plan was solid until I heard what sounded like a loudspeaker in my ear: *"Get out of the road you stupid fuck! I'd love to just run you over but my Jeep's too nice! Get out of the way you loser!"*

What a stupid, one-in-a-million chance. The prick that was veering me into the cars also had a megaphone with speakers set up in his jock-mobile; That alone entitles him to have something bad happen.

I now felt an obligation to mention to him how stupid he was. I waited until we reached the stoplight and rode around to the side of his car. I was about to ask him why the hell he was fucking with me, why he had a loudspeaker in his car, why he couldn't find something else to do on this beautiful day, how stupid his girlfriend was if she was impressed by this shit, etc. but was preempted by him shouting insults and white-kid slang at me. *"You fuckin' loser, get a god damn car. Stay out of the god damn road! Jesus, how old are you, you little bitch, riding that stupid bike around. Stay the fuck out..."*

Well, that's as far as he got. I grabbed his lions' mane of a haircut and whacked his head off the steering wheel, causing the horn to beep and his girlfriend to scream like she was being murdered in a horror movie. *"Why the fuck are you so stupid? Look what you've gotten yourself into! I was LEAVING, dumb fuck..."* BEEP! I bonked his head off the steering wheel again, and by now he was flailing about like he was drowning, hair flying, girlfriend wailing like a lunatic, and people at the upscale café's along the street looking on in bewildered amazement.

At this point he was all but crying, and I hadn't even hit him with anything except his own horn. I told him next time he'd better be sure that the 14-year-old he chose to fuck with was actually 14, gave his head one more resounding thud off the steering wheel, mentioned what an asshole I thought he was, how he'd brought this all on himself, and how I hoped his girlfriend was impressed. She at this point had toned it down to a heaving sob, and he looked as if he had been scared to death, resurrected, and then hit with a small frying pan.

I rode away hastily, realizing that we had created quite a spectacle, and definitely not wanting to explain the very unusual situation to the cops. I was at least five streets down when I turned and watched him sit through the light changes; Twice.

I'm quite sure he got rid of the loudspeaker, and I imagine he and his girlfriend broke up and likely never talked again... Either that or she wore the pants *(and drove the car)* from that day forward.

FATALLY FLAWED

In everyone's day-to-day travels, they surely run across someone that is thinking something bizarre or derogatory about them. One easy way to determine how much of a freak or an asshole someone may be is whether they have the gall to say those things to strangers... I've met more than a few people that haven't yet made the complicated distinction between casual conversation and belligerent antagonism.

The most recent disappointment was a fanatical gentleman at the Home Depot in Lakewood, Ca. My friends were building wooden skateboard ramps, and I was assigned the daunting task of matching the screws they were using to some new ones at Home Depot. I was also responsible for paying for them, carrying the bag to the car, AND delivering them to the builders. All in one day...

I was walking around the worst home improvement store in the free world carrying a screw and looking for the cryptic sign in the aisle that would lead me to its mates when a well-dressed, normal-looking thirty-something man stopped me short. I figured he may have mistaken me for an employee- I get that a lot at establishments frequented by oddballs and older white people- but no such luck.

No question was proposed, merely a statement offered: "*You know, those tattoos are horrible, they look awful.*" OK, I thought for a second, a tattoo purist that found some type of technical imperfections in mine. Constructive criticism- I'm not above it- but again, no such luck.

"*Yeah, you look ridiculous; you should be ashamed of yourself...*" He informed me in a strangely deadpan tone, as if this was a normal walk-in-the-park conversation for him. I took a minute to rebound, and then calmly asked why the fuck he would think I was interested in his opinion of me. "*Well, I don't know why I thought you would be interested, but I felt it was important to bring up. You look ridiculous, and I felt an obligation to tell you.*"

And then he GRINNED at me. HE FUCKING SMILED! After insulting a perfect stranger in an equally strange hardware store, he grinned. So, after squashing my initial desire to break his jaw and then steal his shoes, I formulated my response: "*...so, how about this: if you say one more word to me, I'm going to shove this screw in your neck. So get the fuck away from me, right now.*" All spoken very calmly, and definitely not what he and his inappropriate sense-of-self were expecting to hear.

He put down the brush and bucket of Spackle he was holding very slowly as if I were an officer of the law asking him to relinquish a weapon, and then walked at a fevered pace to the exit of the store. Fuck you. I'm sure he went home to his unfortunate wife and told her that some lunatic at Home Depot threatened his life with no provocation or justification.

Initially I kind of laughed it off, but as it set, it made me mad, frustrated, and discouraged. I always think of behaving in the same ways I want to be treated; If I act like an asshole, then by all means, treat me like one. But on the contrary- I treat others with respect, and that certainly includes strangers and people I've yet to make a tangible impression on.

I guess things of that nature have to happen once in a while to reassure me of the validity of my societal skepticism; I just wouldn't necessarily mind if they happened a little less frequently.

THE WAR

As time lengthens after a notable occurrence or significant feeling, their gravity and severity often dissipate... or at the very least, soften and blur. I believe this is mandatory in order for sanity to stay intact.

I often recall feelings from many years ago as if they were born today, and while I am glad to have had experiences worthy of strong memory, if their potency were to diminish a bit, it would make my psychological situation a little more manageable.

Maybe they are simply un-reconciled within me; Maybe I am just a big fuckin' baby. Either way, when I look around my house at some of the non-disposable things that live there, my eyes often well up and my heart drops. Many other innocuous incidents elicit a similar result.

I am quite sad, quite often. I'm not an overtly morose sort, and certainly not one that needs or solicits sympathy for troubles I have undoubtedly brought on myself. I am also not one that believes being sensitive makes me weak; Quite the opposite. The darkness and ill-ease that keep me up at night also drive me; Sometimes mad, but often times to, through, and past any goals I set or roadblocks that may stand in my way.

And maybe if hard things softened over time, as I wished, it would be a disservice to the memory. Maybe the honor of enduring the experience is served best by its memory staying sharp and mean, and proving useful in guiding my future path.

THE TRUMP CARD

He would stare at the cardboard cutout of a woman (used to market some sort of diet pill) *as if she were going to come alive and adorn him the King of Man.*

I.

Foundation

I was a healthy eater, and had done enough personal homework on the subject that working in a health food store seemed like a great job for an 18-year-old in the midst of trying to figure out where his life would go.

I applied in person, and had an instant report' with the manager, Jim. He loved the mall for the environment, which goes a long way in describing his character; He was *quite* a character. He picked up on my non-slapstick sense of humor immediately, and we got along swimmingly. A perfect cross between Higgins from Magnum P.I. and any other trim, well-kept, mustachioed incarnation of an English butler, his sarcastic smile and scowl were interchangeable, and both were used as methods of passing judgment on every customer, passerby, and employee in our mall.

Jim had a long history in retail management, and even a brief stint as the owner of a video store. That wealth of experience enabled him to work just hard enough not to draw unnecessary attention to himself, and still shine brightly in the face of upper management in-person. He was a low-level management wunderkind, and would not hesitate to tell you so.

Daytime at the mall is often a dead time, and conversation becomes vital so as to not look like you're doing nothing. Jim and I often talked about his numerous ideas for inventions *(all of which he was going to patent at some point)*, and also movies- he watched, critiqued venomously, and lived vicariously through the silver screen.

Prior to my new job, I had interned at a local paper as a staff writer, and was sent to the movies several times a week to watch and review... Jim was jealous, and I think that having held such a prestigious and sought-after position as an unpaid movie reviewer for a sub-par local paper caused him to consider me a peer and not a subordinate.

The only other employee at the store was a very un-noteworthy college girl who up and left with no notice, leaving us searching hastily for a replacement.

Mark Christie was the 3rd person interviewed, and arrived at the mall in a suit and tie.

I know this because Jim would conduct interviews on the benches in the middle of the mall, just to assure that everyone knew he ran the store we worked in. Mark came in, addressed Jim as *"Sir"*, and outside of the get-up, looked about as ordinary as one could look. He looked *notably* ordinary. Light brown hair, 5'7- 5'8, undefined features, slightly pudgy build- not fat, but not fit.

Mark had no knowledge of health food, vitamins, or customer service. He had worked prior at an industrial refrigeration facility in the city as a security guard, and was looking for a job in the mall because his wife worked at a kitchen store there, and they only had one car. Jim was sold.

Ordinary, polite, non-threatening family man.

Hired.

II.

Time, management

Free time was no commodity in most mall jobs. Save the one day per week that we would receive vendor orders and have to unpack, count, tag, and shelve all the items, the daily rigors were limited to dealing with occasional customers and straightening when they left. Simple? Depends who you ask, I guess.

Mark made it known quickly *(and without intention)* that he had no concept of *"neat vs. messy"*, and also no concept of, in a store filled with thousands of tiny bottles, the importance of knowing what went where. His *"straightening"* often looked like a Rorschach test, and it became apparent very quickly that the suit he wore to work every day was but a deception- overdressing, he must have hoped, may mask his incompetence.

Ordinary, maybe, but *normal...* not even close.

The day's conversations were always interesting, and Jim and I were in agreement that Mark's contributions were a case of the bland of the bunch telling tall tales to impress his new associates. Tales of philandering and womanizing, burglary, drunk driving... depraved acts of animal cruelty... ... ... assault on the weak... We believed about half of the stories- the suburb that Mark had grown up in lent itself to early adult petty crime and alcohol abuse. A much better storyteller than he was a mall store employee, Mark's performance did not improve- not even a little bit- in the entire two months since he had been hired.

I had many occasions to work side-by-side with Mark due to the fact that there needed to be two people on per shift, and there were only three of us. We got along OK, and the message that he liked me was made clear when he started talking to me openly about his relationship. His wife was very plain and pretty, but looked very, very, sad. Her face was always hidden under mounds of long, curly, dirty blonde hair, and her nails were always bitten to the quick and often band-aided. They had a two-year-old boy that her parents looked after while they worked at the mall, and she would often bring him in a stroller when they came to pick Mark up at shift's end. She was friendly, and I think she could tell that I did not judge her, as she would mention various things about my appearance, notice if I had changed my hair, gotten new shoes, etc.

After three months of working with Mark I had developed a strange sympathy for her, because it was obvious at every turn that there was only so bright his star was ever going to shine. Those feelings deepened during conversations about his sneaking out to strip clubs, hiding pornography in the most obscure of places, and his fixation on women... all but the one he was married to. To be even-handed, I do not believe he was cheating, but that simply may have been due to the occasion not arising. More than once there was mention of one particular dancer that he was SURE was flirting with him, and there were several female mall employees that were, at a basic level, flattered by his constant staring and attempts at conversation. As soon as one was struck however, their interest waned at once. *"Ordinary"* was no longer a term I would use to describe Mark Christie.

III.

Discovery

There was a palpable level of tension in the mall and surrounding communities that was making mall work even more tedious, and making our already finicky customer base almost unbearable. For the better part of two weeks, a four-year-old girl named Kali Poulton had been missing, and it had put the entire county in a state of alert. It would be impossible not to feel sympathy for the parents and some general hostility towards the entire situation, however the general public channeling those frustrations and fears towards whoever crossed their path was only making everyone more upset. Police presence was intense for the first month of the ordeal, and due to the confusing nature of it all, other states were brought in as well as some national press outlets. There were posters of Kali on every highway, video on every news channel, and flyers in every window of every store in our mall, and all others in the area. Conversations shifted from the mundane and boring to the timely and confusing... *How could someone just walk off with a 4-year-old? Was it the parents? No one saw anything? What is society coming to?*

The environment was somber, and it affected everyone.

IV.

The un-closable door

Women, even as an inanimate form on a pill bottle, had become an almost singular topic of conversation when Mark was involved. From the teenagers that worked in the bookstore across the way, to the women pictured on the sports nutrition products, very little else seemed to be present in the front of his mind.

Regarding private matters and our personal lives, Jim and I were both very guarded... One afternoon Jim gazed upon a very handsome man for the entire length of his walk through the mall, obviously smitten, and that is the only reason I ever would have considered his orientation. Jim's privacy, and my being an 18-year-old only having had one girlfriend, made the daily forays into Mark's dysfunctional sexual psyche very challenging to deal with. One solution Jim came up with was to schedule himself with me almost exclusively, leaving my shifts overlapping with Mark's, and broadening my exposure to him and his family. The morose character of his young wife intensified, and even visually, there was a darkness to her that was new, and growing.

Story time this week included a riveting tale of deceit and deception: In order to spend the entire day at the strip bar, Mark told his wife that he was going to a training seminar, took the day off, took the family car, and sat- for what he told us was almost nine hours- at the Klassy Kat... a far from high-brow gentlemen's club. I was sworn to secrecy, and that was very difficult for me, because I did not particularly like Mark, and I was always glad to speak with his wife for the brief moments she was present. My criticism of the day squandered at the 'Kat evoked a defense mechanism in him... and he challenged *"Aw, that's NOTHING... My friend and I killed and buried an old woman in a gulley out in Hilton a while back. We were hunting and saw her and just decided to do it."*

From a stranger, a disclosure such as that would be very shocking and upsetting, but somehow from Mark- someone I knew better than I'd like to- I took it as a very demented, flawed, cry for attention. *"Wow",* I replied. *"Playing hooky to go to a strip bar IS nothing compared to that."* Pleased that he had *"impressed"* me, he responded *"Yeah, like I said... That was nothing. No one even knows about that but you and Jim... My friends and I, we were crazy. That's NOTHING."*

Jim and I talked many times in those few weeks about Mark, and came to the unscientific conclusion that he was just a dunce, and talked mostly just to hear himself speak.

His work performance was consistent, and poor. Attendance was fine, very simply because he was at the mall a majority of each day whether on shift or not in order to shuttle his wife. I had only seen his son a handful of times but never once had he stood, walked, or crawled out of the stroller, nor had he ever made a sound.

One of the most notable and maddening oddities that had developed in Mark's behavior was a strange, smug smirk that would appear like clockwork whenever his work was called into question, his performance was critiqued, or a mistake he had made was pointed out. All too familiar at that point with his own sub-par performance, the irony of his expression and handling of rebuke was that he made NO effort whatsoever to correct the behavior, or even perform the mentioned task successfully the next time through.

The demeanor of his wife was becoming easier to understand every day that passed with Mark as a co-worker. If the attitudes, smugness, and ambivalence that he exhibited at work were any indications of how he behaved in actual life, I feel that her level of composure was admirable... and her loyalty and love for him must be very strong. Even being subjected to him in small blocks of time made me anxious, confused, and most of all concerned for their poor little boy.

V.

The reckoning

Outside of my job at the mall, I was in daily contact with very few people; I have always kept a small circle of friends. At that point I had just moved out on my own, and was living in the city of Rochester on Culver Road. I was welcomed to my new home in the city with a car burglary, and several days later bore witness to a man being beaten in an alley with a hammer. My mind was filled with thoughts of brutality, violence, and most of all confusion towards all aspects of the environment in which I existed.

I was constantly tense, and was beginning to dread work- not for work's sake, but for the heirs that needed to be put on for my entire shift to avoid confrontation with Mark.

Sympathy existed within me, but it was quickly changing into intolerance and spite.

The Kali Poulton case was still being feverishly investigated, and it added a constant element of tension to all interpersonal situations. No matter what other subject need be discussed, Kali seemed to come up immediately, and everybody had a theory. My sorrow and sympathy for the family was significant, but I was also aware that my opinions on the matter were irrelevant, and talking about it only made me upset.

Jim would speak on it daily, and almost constantly. He had built it up as the demise of society's conscience, and I tended to agree with him. Like most other topics he felt strongly about, he was animated in his telling of simpler times when he was young, where doors were left open, possessions were borrowed and shared with no reservation, and guilt over wrongdoing would prompt an apology and restitution.

I was only 18, but I knew beyond any doubt that those days were gone and would not return.

Our little health food store in the mall had gone from a relatable, well-suited job to an emotional and challenging burden for me. Although I enjoyed talking with Jim, I was developing a strong dislike for Mark. My focus upon entering the mall doors every day began with ways to avoid conversations with him, and then quickly transitioned into thoughts of his wife, who had become a veritable mute for all I could tell, and looked as if she had been awake for months.

Mark was eager to talk to me when I arrived at work. Like a small child trying to keep a secret, he baited me with trivial small talk, all the while grinning like a fool and obviously bursting to tell a story. I began busywork immediately, and he followed, uninterrupted in his quest. *"I was driving on Turk Hill last night and you'll never guess what happened!"* *"No"* I said *"I probably won't."* *"I hit a fucking DEER. Fucking thing came out of nowhere. Luckily it was a small one, and didn't do too much to the car."*

"I am really sorry to hear that. Are your wife and son OK?" I asked, as if that were what he cared about, or wanted to tell me. *"Oh, they were at home. The deer, man, that thing was still alive. It ran off the side of the road... I had to drag it back behind the car and drive over it for a while to make sure it was dead. I've never driven over anything that big; you could really feel it crush under the tires."*

I decided at that moment I was going to be unable to work with Mark any longer. His story gave me the tight, pointed urgency often felt right before entering into a physical confrontation, and the feeling did not lessen the entire shift. I truly felt that with even the slightest future provocation I would attack and beat Mark where he stood. He was the embodiment of everything I tried to avoid in my personal life, and my patience with it had reached an end.

VI.

Descent

I was actively pursuing a transfer to a branch of our store in a mall across town, much to the disappointment of Jim, and the confusion of Mark. He was much too immersed in his unsettling fantasy world to think, even for a second, that he could be a factor in my sudden decision to leave a good job with a boss I liked in a location that made sense.

There was a position available across town, and I took it. Two more weeks and Mark Christie would be nothing more than an odd story to tell my friends.

Jim was upset that I was leaving, and made sure that he let me know by scheduling Mark from the beginning to end of all my shifts, leaving him to work by himself in the mornings. Mark's wife had taken ill, forcing him to ask me for a ride home from work. I said yes, knowing that his wife would have had to come after him at 9:45pm- sick, and with little boy in tow- if I had declined.

As I drove, Mark talked. School, friends, jobs- not one topic did he have a healthy or *"normal"* outlook on. His previous job *(security at the refrigeration facility)* he enjoyed- mostly because of the isolation, and *"power"*, as he called it. He mentioned he had only been back once to drop something off since he quit in order to seek work at the mall. His home was in a small suburb- a yellow condo in a cul-de-sac, front yards filled with children's toys as far as the eye could see. He thanked me for the ride, muttered something about his car, and reminded me that I would see him tomorrow.

I did not want to see where he lived, I did not want to hear what he thought, and I did not want to know what he knew. I struggled through the last two weeks of our time together, and it was one of the only times in my life where trouble in my mind kept me from sleep. I was truly sad to leave Jim- not only was he an interesting person and a friendly, good natured boss, but I felt sympathy and guilt for leaving him to deal with Mark on his own. I questioned his ability to tolerate the situation, and assumed that Jim would end up letting him go very shortly after I left.

The staff at the new store consisted mostly of college kids, as it was in an area littered with everything from prestigious universities to small religious schools. Our district manager was a handful- an ex-jock with a temper and a God complex- but he seemed like an angel of mercy compared to the situation I had just left. Things were good, and due to a departure at the store shortly after my arrival, I was made manager within the month.

The environment I lived in outside of work was hard and cold. I was quickly learning that the area of the city I lived in, although neat and tidy from the outside, was dangerous and required constant attention and vigilance. My free time was taken up with movies, occasional social outings, and bike riding. I worked a lot; Mark Christie, Jim, and my time at the health food store were never far from my mind.

The week after I was promoted to manager of the new store, I received a call from Jim that confirmed my suspicions- he was unable to deal with the stories and dark recollections from Mark's past, and let him go. Jim mentioned that he took it well, smiling throughout the process, and saying *"I understand, I know I wasn't very good at my job."* The maturity with which Mark handled the situation surprised both of us, and we were both also very glad that he was going to be out of our lives. Jim and I both spent a lot of time thinking on, talking about, and dissecting people's character... and we were both made very uneasy by Mark's presence. At any rate: Adios, and good riddance.

VII.

Absolution

Winter had come, and the challenges of everyday life are magnified when winter hits like it does in Rochester, NY. It was a warm social time filled with family and food, and there was a general sense of ease, as even the most devious seemed to be distracted by the approach of a festive season.

I was working long hours at the new store, and spending my off time with family and friends at my apartment in the city. Interpersonal challenges arose frequently at the new store, but I harbored a strange gratefulness towards Mark for making them all seem manageable, and even trivial. It had been almost four months since I had seen or talked to Mark. In that same block of time, I learned that Jim had been hired as a manager in a local movie theater. Knowing how important that position was to someone such as Jim, I extended as hearty a congratulations as I would have if someone I knew had won the lottery, or been made president of a company. Jim could hardly contain his excitement, offered me free movie passes whenever I chose, and thanked me for my friendship at the health food store.

It was a good feeling, and a warming relief that such a confusing and troubling chapter had come to an end in a satisfying way. I did not expect to talk to Jim again, and I think he felt the same. We were friends of situation and circumstance, and without the fodder of the mall and its' inhabitants, our conversations would stand still.

Holiday time brought out the seasonal help in the mall stores, which allowed me several extra evenings a week to myself. A visit from my grandma was timed perfectly, and after my parents brought her to the city to see my apartment, she and I stopped at the grocery store to pick up some last-minute items on the way to my parents' house for a meal. Joined arm-in-arm, we moved slowly through the busy, slippery store, picking several items and pausing often in order to ensure we both made it out of the crowd standing.

Upon stopping at a checkout line, I heard someone call to me in a familiar voice. As I looked left, Mark Christie walked towards us, dressed unconvincingly for the inclement weather, and obviously excited to see me. After exchanging formalities, I introduced him to my grandma *(I don't think he would have left until I did so)*, bid his family my best, and said goodbye. Immediately upon his approach, my chest tightened and my arms prickled just as they had the day he told the story of the deer. I was upset to have introduced him to someone I care about, and was also upset that he had now re-entered my mind.

Casually explaining to my grandma that Mark was an ex co-worker and leaving it at that allowed me to keep to myself the uneasiness that his presence had caused. It stayed with me all the way to my parents' house, and then thankfully, did not return.

It was almost six months later when it- *"it"* being all the angst, suspicion, dread, concern, questioning, morbid curiosity, and confusion ever associated in my mind with Mark Christie- returned, and would never leave me again.

I was sitting in my apartment watching Channel 13, one of three channels I had reception on, and half-reading a magazine. The voice of a female reporter began talking about the Kali Poulton case, and I listened as if eavesdropping while I continued to read.

"...A suspect has been detained in the kidnapping and murder of four-year old Kali Ann Poulton of Penfield. 24-year old Mark John Christie has been arrested and charged with the kidnapping and strangulation of the four-year-old, who was reported missing on May 23rd of 1994. The body was recovered under Christie's direction at a refrigeration plant on Atlantic Avenue in Rochester. Christie was a neighbor of the little girl, and admitted to kidnapping her while she was riding her tricycle and strangling her to death with his bare hands that same night, fearful that her mother would be upset that Kali had been inside his house..."

I listened, and shook, and PRAYED that it was someone else with the same name that had lived in that same city. My denial was squashed conclusively several seconds later when a mug shot eerily similar to our health food store ID photos flashed on the screen, confirming what I can only describe as a point in my memory in which I can recall every single solitary feeling, thought, color, and sound.

Mark Christie- a man who I had worked with almost every day, driven home to the very house where he had done the deed, interacted with the poor wife that had at last turned him in, and who had confessed what I thought at the time to be a made-up murder of an old woman in a river bed- had kidnapped and murdered a harmless, helpless, beautiful four-year-old girl.

I was physically paralyzed, but my mind was electric with thoughts of timelines, feelings of guilt and pain, confusion, panic, sadness, and abject horror.

The situation felt impossible, however at the same time, felt almost logical.

Human instinct is truly a mystery, and yet sadly, it often holds truth and clarity that people are afraid to find or fail to see. Jim and I both KNEW there was something not right, not normal, and not SAFE about Mark, but we did nothing more than discuss it amongst ourselves. I was overwhelmed with fury, and simultaneously rendered immobile with sadness and guilt.

It took upwards of an hour for me to move from my perch on the couch. The news had ended and Entertainment Tonight had started. I could not look away, as if I were waiting for a retraction to flash on the screen, or to wake up from an unintentional early evening nap. My first clear thought was that I had to call Jim.

Acting in auto pilot, I looked up the phone number to the theater where he was now manager, and slowly dialed the number, hoping with all my heart that he was not at work.

A boy answered, and I asked to speak with the manager. Jim took the line, just as he had at our health food store. *"This is Jim Garling speaking, how can I help you?"* *"Jim... it's Greg."* *"Greg! How are you? Are you calling to take me up on those movie passes?"*

"No Jim... Mark Christie killed Kali Poulton."

VIII.

Elevator, going down...

"WHAAAT?!?! How do you know that you motherfucker? That is NOT a funny joke! JESUS CHRIST GREG!" Jim was beside himself, and refused to believe that I was serious. *"Jim, I would never joke about such a thing. I am so sorry, I wanted to tell you right away, because I knew you would be as upset as..."* ...I then heard banging and crashing, screaming, and Jim carrying on in the background of the phone, which he had either dropped or put down. *"JIM! Jim... are you there? JIM? I'm sorry!"* *"Mister?"* *"Yes, I'm here."* I said.

"Jim just took off man. He seemed upset, and he just left. His shift isn't over for 3 hours."

"Thanks. Goodbye"

The city was in a state of agitation and alarm, as the largest child kidnapping case in its history had been wrapped up- the guilty being a man who lived less than 100 yards from the victim; A man that had commented to her mother about *"her attractive little girl"*, a man that shared a playground with her, and had a youngster of his own.

I had not left my house in three days, unable to come to grips with the reality that was everywhere I looked. I had been contacted by the local news station for a comment; Apparently when looking through his employment history my name was in there as well, along with a phone number. I denied the woman an on-camera interview, but told her she could quote me as saying *"Mark Christie is a fucking psycho, and although I was surprised to see that he had kidnapped Kali, it was not surprising that he had done something horrible, as he was nothing but a self-centered piece of shit. All the sympathy in my heart goes to Kali's family, and to Mark's wife and young son."*

In the week following, I would learn that the woman he had told the story of killing in the riverbed in Hilton was, in actuality, his first victim. I vomited when I saw the news on the television, and felt immediately that if I had been more in tune with what I was being told, I could have reported it and possibly averted further disaster. I was sick with disgust, both towards Mark and towards myself for making an assumption about such a grave and serious situation that was put before me. In looking back on my pay stubs from the little health food store in the mall, I also learned that I had worked alongside Mark on May 22nd and May 24th of 1994.

All the idiosyncrasies related to Mark Christie were now so clear... The statement that he had only been back once to the site of his old job to *"drop something off"*... The darkness that seemed to be overtaking his poor wife... His entire fantastical, fake existence- removed as far as possible from his real, twisted, life...

Most of all though was his knowing, smug, smile that appeared whenever things were not going his way. A smirk as pompous as any I've ever seen, as if to tell us that he was too good for this world, that he knew more than we ever could... and that he held the trump card, only to be seen when he chose to reveal it.

IX.

The End

I had called the movie theater several times over the next few weeks, and Jim had not returned to work since the night of my first call. I had finally left the house, but was a virtual zombie; For the first and only time in my life, nightmares based on reality had interrupted my sleep to the point of insomnia.

It is now 2007- 13 years after I met Mark Christie- and I can say beyond a shadow of a doubt that I think of him more than all of my childhood friends and teachers combined. The details of this story, and the few incidentals that I did not have written notes on, are as fresh in my mind as my most recent meal, and the guilt I feel for playing a complacent bit-part in Mark's fucked up life has settled permanently into a nice, warm place in my gut.

East Rochester still watchful

At school and at play, children are subjects of

Case strewn with mayhem and whites

FLYING[1]

I backhanded a guy on a plane returning from Los Angeles not too long ago. I was reluctant to tell the story because it could make me seem like some sort of short-fused prick, which really isn't true, but it *is* pretty nuts and just illustrates how unnecessarily fussy people can be.

I was sitting next to a very nice, very attractive, upscale woman probably in her early 30's and much to my surprise, she talked to me pretty consistently throughout the flight. She was interesting enough that I didn't realize the flight was arriving late and I only had five minutes to reach my connection; Once I did I immediately stepped into the aisle and, continuing our conversation, so did she.

Sitting catty-corner from us was a guy drinking Jack & Coke's, and reading a book about the '70's TV show "BJ & the Bear"; "BJ" being a man, "Bear"

---

[1] Originally published in "Dig" Magazine, 1999.

being a monkey, and the series being one of the worst I've ever accidentally witnessed. The man bumped and shoved his way into the aisle, apparently still pissed about the cancellation of the show two decades earlier. After being pushed into the seats a few times, my seatmate asked him very politely if he would mind waiting a minute to get settled because she was getting hit every time he moved.

"I've got to put my STUFF in my BAG so I can get off the PLANE! Jesus." A few minutes later, after pushing her a bit more and clipping her with his bag from the overhead compartment, she asked again if he could possibly wait a minute to thrash around. *"FUCK YOU BITCH"* he says, and then glares at her for having the audacity to speak to him again.

After taking a minute to compose herself, the woman said calmly *"I really feel sorry for people that have no control over their anger."* *"...WHO the FUCK... blah blah blah... SHUT UP BITCH... blah blah blah... I'll do whatever the..."* Finally I say *"Hey man, wind it down. We all have to stand here for a while, no reason to make it worse."* He responds *"YOU PRICK, WHAT THE... blah blah blah... JUST FUCK OFF!"*

In a final swing at diplomacy, I offer *"Listen, please wind it down. No one wants to hear you swearing at everyone..."* ... but no such luck. *"YOU GOT AN ISSUE WITH ME, YOU PRICK? FUCK YOU!"* And in true '70's TV style, he winds up and shoves me, flop-top hair flying, swearing all the while. I blinked for one second and then used the hand not on my bag to crack him squarely in the head. His sunglasses flew off, he fell into the seat behind him, and as he started gathering steam to get back up, I stared at him, pointed to the seat, and quietly told him to sit the fuck down until I got off the plane.

The stewardesses were trying to contain their laughter, my seatmate was trying to get off the plane as quickly as possible, and my next awareness was running through the airport and realizing that I had just smacked a stranger on an airplane.

Maybe he learned a lesson, but it's likely all he was thinking is that he should have hit me first.

FAG IN THE POOL

If I got paid by the word for stories about assholes fucking with me, I'd be writing this one from the 3rd floor of my Hollywood Hills condo, overlooking the entire hazy human petting zoo that is the city of Los Angeles.

I'm in Long Beach. I don't really blend here, per se', but I feel I do my best. I walk around and keep to myself, eat at many of the same places on a weekly basis, drink these froofy blended coffee drinks with funny names like *"Freddo"*, and yet, in my sincere desire to fly under the radar, things often go awry.

Partially my fault in this particular situation, I admit; I visit a fairly upscale gym here in Long Beach once or twice a week. It's walking distance from my house, and slightly more expensive than 24-Hour Fitness or something, but I'd spend the difference in fuel and frustration if I had to drive.

I walk over, row in place for 20 or 30 minutes with headphones on, converse briefly with the few people there that don't think they're better than me and everyone else walking the earth, and occasionally sit in the hot tub.

Two factors played more than a small part in the unfolding of this story:

1. Gay marriage has been a big issue this year; If that is news to you, you should be somewhere besides here catching up on national news.

2. I usually don't go in the hot tub when there are a bunch of idiots hanging around it, but I was banged up, and decided to go against my better judgment in the interest of feeling less so.

At the risk of getting too racy, I will simply say that bathing suits are optional in this particular gym hot tub situation; A lot can be learned very quickly about someone by how they handle this. For example: If you are squatting around the edge sans bathing suit while there are other people in the hot tub, you are inconsiderate, confusing, and disgusting.

Today there were a handful of guys in the hot tub that seemed to be friends; They all come to the gym together and then jump in the tub after their lat pull-downs and wax political. Lucky me.

I was definitely looking forward to my time in there, as it is one of a very few things that helps me feel like I am not riddled with arthritis and about to enter a state of atrophy.

Today's bathing topic. Gays in the military, gay marriage, gays, gays, gays. In retrospect, I imagine the fervor in which the leader of the goof troop was conveying his warped position was in fact a very clear insight into the true feelings he harbored towards his little buddies. I should have mentioned that to him.

"Gay marriage is just ridiculous. How can you expect to live normally just because you're married? Not to mention, it's like, where will it end? Can you marry your cousin next?"

"People just choose to be gay so they can have a cause to rally for. I know SOOO many people that say they're gay now, but I'm sure when they were younger they were as straight as you and I."

(At this point, unintentionally, I began looking suspiciously at the talker, since he obviously had some serious issues to handle...)

"I just don't get it... you're not BORN gay... there's no way! It's like saying that everything else is right, but trying to convince everyone that you just somehow like people of the same sex? There no way God would make people gay, since he says it's wrong in the bible."

"I mean, gays in the military are just kind of looking for trouble. I guess if they're there, and

they keep to themselves, it's OK, but the military is no place for people that think like that..."

(At THIS point I may or may not have snickered and shaken my head, which, in his animated state may have not been amusing to Jock Gestapo- I'm pretty sure that was his name...)

OK, I DEFINITELY snickered and UNINTENTIONALLY shook my head, and J.G. noticed. He nudged one of his friends, laughed, and then said to me, brilliantly, *"You got a problem?"*

I offered a sardonic smile, and shook my head no.

He paused, began to look very pleased with himself, and said

"Hey guys, I think we've got a FAG in the POOL!"

He chuckled, his friends looked a bit uneasy, I took a moment to reflect, and then as I slowly stood up and grabbed my towel, said *"I'm much less confused about THAT than I am about how four PUSSIES found their way into the MENS locker room!"*

Oooohh, I called them PUSSIES... ooooohh, aaaaaaahhhh, sssssshhhhh...

The already-uncomfortable cohorts tittered nervously, and of course J.G. had to defend his non-gay, 100% American stud-muffin image by throwing something back: *"You faggot, you calling me a pussy? Do you have any IDEA...?"* Argh, that was just about enough of that. I went into emergency overdrive, realizing that I had just insulted four grown men, by myself, naked, in a hot tub.

He was still talking shit, his friends were obviously nervous, and I stood at the side of the tub in a towel and calmly told them that I would smash at least two of their heads in before the other two got at me, and that if they had any desire of ever playing 18 holes of golf again, they should fuck off and leave me be...

The non-enthusiastic associates looked guilty and embarrassed, and J.G looked like he was going to give it one more shot when one of his bros told him to leave it alone. I'm about 5'11, medium build, and have the word *"vengeance"* tattooed vertically down my sternum from my neck to my belly.

I had never thought of that being an asset of any kind, but I would imagine in this unique and bizarre situation, me, standing wet in a towel, threatening these Monday-morning-quarterback assholes with physical violence, it may have added an element of authenticity.

The curtain call to this unpleasant little display was uneventful. I watched them over my shoulder as I hurried up and got the fuck out of there; They stayed in place, looking stunned and humiliated. And god damn well they should be.

I look at it like this: If you are going to say absurd, inflammatory things in the vein of what

J.G. was spitting out, you need to AT LEAST expect to get looked at sideways. I didn't say anything, I didn't splash him...

He over-reacted, and hopefully at the end of the day at least went home feeling stupid for running his mouth and then acting like a dick when someone within earshot wasn't 100% on board.

Fuck it. The end. I saw one of the guys the next week and he was overwhelmingly friendly, and went out of his way to be so. I was, of course, friendly in return.

Imagine the story if I would have gotten my ass kicked by four guys, by myself, naked, in a hot tub.

I'll have to try harder next time.

HIGHER EDUCATION

This is a story about the day I learned that people don't always truly believe in what they seem to stand for, or actually stand for what they say they believe...

I've always been confused by the college dorm dynamic, probably because I never lived in one. You're supposed to live in close quarters with people you barely know, probably don't altogether like, and yet still learn, study, and stay sane. They should give a degree just for making it through that with a full head of non-grey hair.

The girlfriend of an associate of mine went to college outside Rochester in the exact environment described, and for some fucking reason, we would go hang out there fairly often. It was that or the mall, and there's just so many times you can look at the same shitty selection of records.

Going there was like a sociology experiment. We didn't mesh with what was happening at the school, and were greeted with either pleasant curiosity or unpleasant ferocity- no surprise, the line between interested and hostile was largely gender-based. Insecure, unoriginal college boys don't want anyone honing in on their turf; I've got another story about that later.

We'd sit around, walk around, I fell asleep a few times on the comfy couches in the lounge- but mostly we'd chat with whoever was on study break, and usually it was the girlfriends' roommate. For the sake of discussion, we'll call her Jodi. Jodi was *(I say "was" because she was a wishy-washy pseudo-intellectual snob who is now, I'm sure, whatever her rich husband wants her to be...)* into Amnesty International, being vegetarian, and most adamantly, not drinking. In hindsight, her staunch and vocal "non-drinker" campaign was probably just a way for her to feel unique and different in an environment that was decidedly neither.

Drinking was the word of the day for most of the other people on campus. Two or three nights a week the girls would traipse off to some Caribbean-themed nightclub to hang around with college types and in Jodi's case, vocally not-drink. To each his own, but I'd have to be sedated to hang around in a place like that with a bunch of pretentious college kids. But I guess when you ARE a pretentious college kid, it's hard to see the forest for the trees.

Anyway.

My friend and I were on our standard weekend route through the college expecting to hang around with our usual suspects, only to find out that it was some sort of college holiday and there was to be a mass-exodus to a bar on the other side of town. We sure as fuck weren't going, and just as surely didn't have anything else to do besides play Sega hockey at his cold apartment or get into trouble somewhere, so we resolved to go read magazines at the grocery store and come back around the time of their expected return. Exciting, right? When not traveling for BMX or hardcore... welcome to most of my young adult life. And the girls we were coming back to see weren't even cool.

We read magazines, had thorough and highly intellectual discussions about their content, watched people come in and out of the video store for a while, and then made our way back to college. We came up on a herd of girls surrounding Jodi, who was sobbing uncontrollably, and another girl that looked upset but not quite so unhinged... not a usual scene after a night of carefree college debauchery.

In between hysterics, it was discovered that a guy *(I think his name was Mark, or Mike, who fuckin' cares)* got behind the wheel of the car the girls were riding home in, completely fucking obliterated. Their story was that he couldn't even keep his head up, but somehow thought it wise to drive 25 minutes home from college asshole night at the bar. The girls continued the story, which included him yelling at them for implying he couldn't handle himself behind the wheel, him laughing at their sobbing pleas to pull over, veering into lawns, and finished with him running over some sort of small animal on one of the rural roads surrounding the campus.

As the story continued to unfold, the other girl began to cry, which made Jodi cry harder and eventually hype. Obvious questions were asked, such as why the fuck they didn't get out of the car when he stopped at a light, etc. but like many situations, unless you're there it is impossible to pass judgment.

I'm not winning any humanitarian awards, but this case felt too close to home to not do something. Those girls were completely traumatized by an inconsiderate college *"friend"* willing to risk their lives for the sake of a drunken ego. My friend and I were pissed. We too were non-drinkers, I still am, and so the thought of being put in danger by something you don't even yourself take part in is maddening. Looking back, I'm glad the people in the dorms refused our requests for his room number. It was better to have some time to let emotions cool down.

We were told by the girlfriend that Jodi was fairly distraught for the days following the incident. I was upset about it as well. It didn't happen to me, but I couldn't and still can't understand how someone could think for a second *(even in an intoxicated state)* that it is OK to put someone in such a situation, especially in spite of strong protest.

As per usual, Wednesday we ended up back at college. There was a small lounge area right in front of the girls' room where we frequently hung out. It was drab: Off-white walls, dirty tan couches, and used-to-be burgundy carpet. There was also an odd fake fire fireplace like you'd see in a model home. We were hanging out talking and two kids we didn't recognize walked up. One immediately went in to talk to Jodi; The body language and mannerisms she exhibited when he entered the room made me immediately aware that he was the one driving the other night. She all but refused to converse with him, so he came out into the lounge to enlist us as sympathizers.

In addition to my friend and me, his girlfriend and another girl from the floor were sitting on the couches. The driver began talking shit about how people freak out over nothing, he's done that a million times and nothing has happened, and the closer- *"It's like when a girl says no to sex: she really doesn't mind, she just doesn't want to admit it."*

Too much. I'm curious what he ended up with a degree in. I'm sure it has something to do with combining large dough circles, big metal ovens, and tomato paste.

I've had many occasions to, but I am proud to say that I have only COMPLETELY lost my temper a very few times... this being one of them. The kid was my size, but soft from being a lush and a computer geek. As soon as I grabbed him I felt him tense up and make fists, and as I started shaking him I could feel him panic. I had a hold of his lapel and the back of his head. I was more or less shaking him to keep him from getting a good shot at me, all the while explaining to him the finer points of why I disagreed with his choices the previous weekend. My friend made damn sure his friend didn't have any wild notions to intervene, and the girls jumped up on the couches as if there was some sort of rodent on the ground. The kid got slapped a few times, not really hit at all, but I was really fucking upset. I still to this day don't know why this instance struck such a nerve, but it sure did.

As I mentioned, he was my size, and I'm not sure physically how it happened, but I threw him completely over one of the couches hard enough that his back and arm cracked an imprint in the wall where he hit. Just like 90% of the times I've been in physical altercations I didn't feel any better afterwards.

I don't think I expected the girls to be happy that I had gone after the kid, but I definitely did not expect the response I got: They were appalled- Jodi especially. They were swearing at me, telling me never to come back, etc. and I couldn't believe it. We went and sat downstairs while the girls composed themselves... we should have just left.

They came down to talk to us a little while later and were still pissed. I explained that I was as upset by his attitude regarding the situation as the situation itself. I said that if people like that think what is said to them is a joke, they are going to take advantage of people their whole life, and I wanted to show him that there can be real-life repercussions to taking advantage.

Yeah... that didn't make any sense to Jodi, who then confoundingly proceeded to prove his girls/sex point: Now that the situation is over, she said, she realized that she could have done things differently and that he was just trying to get her attention.

Holy mother of shit; He's the victim, and all of a sudden they are thinking that I just beat up the victim! Is that what college does to people? Critical thinking is so over-emphasized yet so misunderstood that what she came up with seemed to them like a sane, sensible rationalization.

Synopsis:

An adamant non-drinker gets essentially forced into a car ride with a severely intoxicated man who is driving very dangerously. He will not let them out even though they are crying and pleading with him. The result is a very upset girl and very concerned friends of the girl.

The driver is a complete fucking idiot scumbag and can't even admit his wrongdoing and move on. In addition, he says classic frat-boy date rape shit that seals his fate. I slap him and toss him around the room, fairly diplomatically and with very little damage to anything but his ego, which needed a bit of damaging.

All of it somehow equates to me being an asshole that is completely out of line, and the girl feeling sorry that she didn't hear his cries of social distress masked by blatant disregard for the safety and well-being of others. This also leaves the girl contemplating how SHE could have handled the situation differently, and the worthless loser that caused the whole thing learning no lesson other than the fact that he should learn how to fight.

Ugh.

I don't understand being complacently *"against"* something. The girl had ranted and raved on many occasions prior to this whole debacle about how bad drinking was, how it was messing her friends up, they were failing out of school, etc. Then when the time comes to ACTUALLY BE AGAINST IT and to make a statement, she instead makes excuses and blames herself for being closed-minded.

I am of the other persuasion. If something is worth being against, it's worth fighting for, physically or otherwise. I thought this was a situation where that mentality would be embraced, since this involved total disrespect and potentially serious harm to a friend. I guess I overestimate peoples' dedication to the words they speak and the ideas they convey. It's a mistake I had made before this happened, and certainly one I've made since.

I guess now is as good a time as any to start doubting the sincerity of what people say; It's probably long overdue.

You know, maybe I AM the idiot. I've just always wanted to support what my friends believe in, trust what they say, and fight for them when I need to. I guess it's a character flaw.

Beginning of the End[1]

What do I believe?

I believe that you will almost always be let down; If you are not, it is the exception, not the rule. I believe that people are generally bad, and if you are lucky enough to find a few truly good ones to associate with, it is the exception, not the rule.

I believe that I will often be disappointed and very seldom surprised; I would rather be sustainably negative and surprised once in a while than eternally positive and disappointed all time.

I believe that trying to live by any ambitious set of standards or strict code of ethics is a frustrating yet worthwhile exercise in futility, since fewer and fewer people each day seem to give a fuck about courtesy or respect.

---

[1] Originally written as an intro to the War of Attrition website when it first went online in January 1999.

I believe that modern society is purgatory; It isn't some mysterious place on the way to Hell. We're fucking there. Right now.

Look around; There's a child-abusing priest in every neighborhood, depravity on every channel, atrocities on every front page, disease on every doorstep, government in every mailbox.

I believe that the days of carefree world-enjoyment are long gone. When I'm at home, I relax. When I walk out my door, I'm always quietly ready for war.

Everyone is out for themselves, everyone is out to belittle thy neighbor. I won't be a target, and I'll never be a victim; I will make a stark example out of any attempt at either.

To this lost-and-soft generation of counter-culture imposters:

Fuck you, and fuck all your friends that aren't going to stick up for you when the real bell tolls. They never really liked you and neither do I.

(Remember: Roaring in the mirror does not make you a lion...).

THE CURSE OF AWARENESS, PART ONE

Many weekends I try to go to the movies. I research the times, plan my pre-movie meal, and venture to the theater usually 15-20 minutes early. Almost every weekend, something off-putting happens in the parking lot or the foyer that prevents me from following through with the viewing. Not *lose sleep* type things by any means; More like, *lose interest.*

People *(with exceptions noted of course),* often confound and frequently sicken me; It might sound cynical and likely a bit clichéd but sadly, the fact remains.

I watch the careless, haphazard way in which they do simple things like park a car, get out, walk to a destination, and enter; Often I am jealous of their lack of awareness, but most times I feel blessed by my own. Often I feel like I have taken too seriously the simplest details of life;

Other times I feel that without doing so, the rest of ones' life could fall to carelessness.

In a brief but impressive run I saw a woman, husband in-tow, grotesquely park her sedan in 1+1/2 spaces, fling the door open and bump the neighboring car, drag a wrapper and a bottle out her door and into the lot upon exiting *(leaving them, of course),* bark something at her poor husband, and walk directly in front of a moving car on her life and death mission to reach the theatre *(of course getting angry with the driver of the moving car).*

Would I have to talk with her in the theatre? *No, of course not.* Were we even planning on seeing the same movie? *Unlikely.* If I could get over myself would I likely have done well with two hours of mindlessness? *Definitely.*

The problem is, I don't *want* to get over it. I don't want to be where "*she*" is... I don't want to do what "*she*" does. I don't want to *see it* just as much, if not more, than I don't want to let it affect me. In a way I'm *glad* it affects me. Feeling the effect is trying, and often makes me feel silly or maladjusted; *Not* feeling the effect would unknowingly make me what I seem to despise. We are often at least pieces of what we despise, though it is worthwhile when discovered to attempt to be otherwise.

If in fact I did not sicken myself in much more profound ways than others ever could, I would feel a fool of another color completely- one casting judgments from a fake ivory tower, thinking their path has not also been riddled with judge-able acts.

To the contrary, I am the pot simply *noticing* that the kettle is black.

Not calling it such, yet keenly aware of the differences in the appearance and execution of life between myself and my would-be theatre mate... Similar only in physical location, we have arrived there by remarkably different routes and with quite polarizing life intentions.

DISAPPOINTED, NOT SURPRISED

Fuckin' California(*ns*).

I was stepping out to cross the street in a very upscale shopping area by my house when an extremely old woman tripped on the curb and fell flat on her face right beside me. I mean *flat*; No hands out, no head turn.

I dropped the bag I was holding, hustled over to her, and carefully picked her up. She couldn't have weighed 75-80 pounds; I have a medicine ball that weighs nearly as much as she did.

She was bleeding from her forehead, nose and mouth, and not doing much else. The area was moderately crowded- I assumed that someone would notice a young person holding a motionless, bleeding old person and immediately offer to help. In the meantime I just stood there and held on to her; I have never held an infant, but I imagine that is what it would feel like. She was light, not just in weight, but in composition. She felt completely fragile, like just-frozen ice.

Eventually, people started coming over and several actually asked *me* what to do. If they had grown up in the same society I had, the obvious path was to call 911 *(which a man was finally courteous enough to get off his other call to do).* Fucking morons.

Moments later this douche in a jean jacket with the collar up and some haircut came over and told me *"Uh, I took some nursing classes in college, and you should definitely be tipping her head back to stop the bleeding".* I promptly took out my 3rd hand and tipped her head back while still attempting to stabilize her quasi-lifeless body. Jean jacket then says *"You know, you should sit her down so she doesn't fall over".* We're on a street corner, not in an auditorium. I don't know where *I'd* sit down right here, and I'm not 100-years-old and bleeding from my head.

"Just sit her down on the ground".

"Uh, don't lean her on that car, her foot is going to slip off the curb".

"Take her into the bank."

FUCK. Does anyone else have a suggestion? It's not like I'm some expert in handling injured senior citizens. I was trying to hold her as still as possible because the way my brain works I assumed that her neck was probably broken and that she was going to die in my arms. She was also still bleeding, and at this point hadn't made a sound or opened her eyes in over five minutes.

What seemed like an hour later a woman who works for the Fire Department came over and renewed a modicum of my faith in humanity. She told me she had seen exactly what happened and had called an ambulance.

She asked me if the woman had lost consciousness, which I was unsure of; Thankfully jean jacket was still there to contribute: *"No, she never lost consciousness... I've done some nursing training, and I can tell you, consciousness was never lost! This man just stood there with her though, so who knows how much blood she's lost. Her head was not tipped back at all."*

The Fire Department lady looked exasperated yet familiar with his type, and asked me to help her put the old woman in a chair some twit from the Gap had brought out. When I looked in the Gap window, there were no less than eight people standing there gawking like they were watching television. God only knows how long they had been standing there, and whether they just stood and stared while I waited for assistance.

Jean jacket started talking loudly about the blood loss to impress the newly gathering crowd, and then thankfully the ambulance showed up. They were asking me and the Fire Department lady about the situation, and jean jacket literally jumped in front and started telling them how he had medical training and he had been monitoring the situation and how I had just been standing there with her and carrying on about how *"...amazing it is that some people don't know even the basics of first aid."*

When they finally took her from me I hustled off and watched from across the street. The ambulance guys finally asked jean jacket to leave, gave the woman oxygen, and then took her away.

Where else but Southern California can you start out helping someone in a bad situation and end up getting condescended by a nursing school dropout Huey Lewis impersonator, while serving as a 15-minute reality show for some nitwit Gap employees?

It could happen elsewhere, I suppose... but it's way more likely in fuckin' Southern California.

The end.

Through, Not Around

'Let the simple have their simple victories...

Our victories of ego need only be over ourselves; Nothing petty demands to be proven through posturing, silly slander or false bravado when you have found and remain on a brave path.

Hold yourself accountable for your stumbles or shortcomings, but share credit with the community that supports you for your triumphs.'

This sentiment can be applied to something as simple as someone racing to pass you in their car, intentionally inconveniencing you at the store, or transparently poking fun at you in a feeble attempt to heal a bruised ego. All are wastes of energy to respond to, and indulging them in any way will often do more to take away from your daily mission than to honor it.

Simple people fight simple battles. It's... *simple.* Skip it.

Be a lion in the path, knowing which harmless creatures to let by, and which to take the effort to devour;

If your intention is to *destroy*, do so with ferocity and malice.

If your intention is to *annoy*, acknowledge the triviality of such acts.

ROAD HAZARD

You'll often hear people romanticize the idea of hitting someone as hard as they can; Those that have done so, however, would very likely tell you that there is nothing romantic about it. The sometimes sickening noise, the way the impact feels inside your own body and head, the blood... And for most, the moments of questioning afterward as to whether that level of severity was warranted.

I didn't feel any anger or post-incident ill-will towards the misguided lot that attempted to steal my bike *(while I was riding it...)* right down the street from my house. All the animosity I was feeling was completely self-directed. It was also justified, and overwhelming. I needed a break from my brain so badly that I chose to go on a bike ride wearing headphones and listening to music- something that under any ordinary circumstances I would never even think of. My life was falling apart, and it was my fault... If I didn't distract myself, it could have easily gotten the better of me. A simple bike ride, close to home, with a little musical accompaniment.

People do it all the time.

I wasn't going anywhere in particular. I had plans to stop at the store at some point and get a snack, and also to ride down one especially great hill that sat just outside the city limits. I was wearing shorts, a t-shirt, and a hooded sweatshirt with the hood up- upon reflection I realized that many of the odd situations I find myself in are a result of what I feel are a gross mis-profiling of my age. I probably looked 17, based both on wardrobe and the fact that I was riding a 24" BMX bike... not bizarre or unprecedented, but also not the most usual mode of transportation for a 30-year-old.

After pedaling standing up for what was probably a half mile, I sat down and began to think about the total fucking mess I had created. No level of volume or amount of simple physical exertion could draw my focus away from what was at hand, or the fact that I had no idea how to fix any of it. I was riding slower than usual, and with my mind totally elsewhere...

My back tire made a familiar noise, and the instinctive thought was simply *"Fuck"*. I've had no less than 1,000 flat tires in my life, and probably 250 of them have happened when I would least prefer, and when they are the most inconvenient. I began to slow down and realized immediately that I was now guilty of my OWN mis-profiling; I did not have a flat tire- Two young adults were kicking my wheel in an attempt to knock me off the bike.

They were riding mountain bikes, and appeared to be in their late teens- old enough to know better, but possibly too close to the suburbs to have ever *learned* better. I stopped abruptly, pulled the headphones off, and stood behind my bike. It was then that I noticed three or four more kids on bikes- with one doubled-up- probably half a mile back. There were words exchanged, the simple nature of which were *"Our friends are coming! Give us that fucking bike!"* and my equally simple refusals. It became clear very quickly that this could end up a huge fucking mess if I did not handle it immediately and efficiently. Fleeing the scene had stopped being a practical option as soon as I had stepped off my bike.

I quickly put the bike down to my side, and as one of the thieves bent down to grab it, I kicked him square across the front of the head with my shin. His head split, as did my leg, and he dropped to the ground as if his batteries had abruptly died. His friend paused briefly, threw his bike down, and came after me. He stumbled and I grabbed on to his shirt and hit him in the face with my elbow until he stopped fighting and fell down. I was bleeding from both my leg and arm... both boys were on the ground, presumably seriously hurt.

The other group was now a mere hundred yards away, and in a foolish attempt to keep all of them from chasing me I threw one of the downed bikes over a guardrail that led to the freeway. I grabbed my bike, ran beside it for a few feet, and then pedaled as fast as I could, assuming that at least a few of them had decided to follow. They were all on mountain bikes, and likely not as proficient on theirs as I was on mine, but the advantage of gears and bigger tires could easily offset the skill level. My brother's house was nearby, and I knew if I made it there I could either hide or fight, and either way I wouldn't be by myself. I turned as often as I could, crossed traffic recklessly, and reached the mid-block house with them just barely having turned down the street. I pounded frantically on the door; My brother answered, and without hearing a word knew exactly what was up. The bike went in the basement, we went on the porch, and we waited.

Crouched down and watching, it wasn't 30 seconds later that the followers rode slowly past the house, taking time to look in the driveways but obviously not having seen exactly which one I turned in to. Once we confirmed them to be safely past the house we went back outside and watched until they turned the corner on to a main road. There were four. Separate from everything else, I was surprised- shocked even- that not even a few of them had stayed to tend to their possibly injured friends. I guess the types that would attempt to steal bikes while people are riding them aren't necessarily the most caring and compassionate.

After seeing which way they turned and cleaning myself up, I called another friend that lived locally and asked him to drive by the bridge- I was equally concerned that the boy I had kicked was dead and that the bike I had thrown over the guardrail had gone on to the freeway. I was anxious for him to report his findings, and in the meantime I pulled the bike back out and resumed my ride... sans headphones, and with significantly more alertness.

I continued my path to the store and got a snack- a slightly more indulgent one than I would have had the afternoon unfolded as originally planned- and very thankfully heard that there was no ambulance, no sign of the boys, and no sign of mayhem on the freeway.

It took more than I would have liked it to, but an attempted bike-jacking followed by a short street fight and capped off with some high-speed urban evasion managed to distract me from myself for a short time. The problem is, the one enemy you can never out-run is fixed permanently right on top of your shoulders, and the pain it can inflict far exceeds anything another person *(or persons)* could ever hand down...

SOUR TIMES

I visited a Target store today in a suburb of Rochester, NY *(no, that's not the end of the story...)*.

It was my day off, and I could not think of a single thing on earth I wanted to do, so my next idea was to do something totally normal and see if that gave any inspiration. I figured I'd walk around, look at about six-million things neither I nor anyone else needs, maybe buy a shirt and a few apples *(they have groceries now, you know...)*, and definitely buy some expensive hand soap.

Shirts went better than I expected. I got a few OK tank tops, they were on sale *(or at least that's what the sign said)* and one of them isn't even black. After trying them on I went back to grab a second one, and came upon some boys.

They were lounging around living-room style in the men's section drinking milkshakes from Starbucks *(they have a Starbucks now, you know...)*, and talking as if they were outdoors trying to speak over a crowd. Most of it was nonsense. They were either going to a state park or Seabreeze later in the day *(Seabreeze is an amusement park here in Rochester that could easily be the setting for the most amazing slasher film ever made)*, and my guess is that either their sisters or mothers were at the store procuring supplies. *"So-and-so might be going, blah, blah, blah, but so-and-so are going to the outlet mall. Kelly is going, but she is SUCH a BITCH! What a total BITCH!"* There was laughter between them, seemingly impressed with themselves for talking like what I expect are their TV heroes. *"Yeah, I mean, she's a total BITCH, and she's not even that hot."* Giggles commenced in a manner that I, as someone that is not opposed to or emasculated by giggling, found to be creepy and very young-girlish.

These were obviously two upper-middle class teenagers from the suburbs that had never *"talked shit"* to anyone but each other, probably hadn't ever sworn in front of an adult *(or a girl)*, and were pretty fucking proud of themselves for doing so.

The curse words were easily twice the volume of the others as if they were being shouted to prove a point.

I was within earshot, and as would be in any North American Target store on a Sunday afternoon, many others were as well. I couldn't care less if those boys burst into flames, the soft stuff melted into a pile of goo, and their skeletons walked out the store holding hands, but there were kids around, and swearing *(especially that kind)* in an involuntary group setting is just trashy. I wasn't in a particularly nurturing mood as I addressed them. *"Why don't you keep your voice down, homie? No one wants to hear you swearing about a girl that's not even here to defend herself. Right?"* I walked within probably six feet of them but had made no eye contact yet. The swearer squeaked a *"Yes"* and the giggler got up off the ground and they stood closely together.

I picked up the second tank top, finally looked right at them *(for a few seconds longer than they were comfortable with, based on their body language)* and then cordially began talking to them about how hard it is to find tank tops that are long enough. They didn't get it at first- I think they were waiting for something worse to happen. I nodded at them, they kind of laughed, and the giggler commented that he knows what I mean because he has a really long torso. *"Now, that's better, isn't it? No reason to carry on like you two were in public, right?"* They nodded, if only in the interest of self-preservation. I was smiling now, so they attempted to do the same, and I walked away.

I'm sure it became a joke not long after leaving the store. The tiny footprint my overbearing, annoying scolding left was no match for the empowerment I saw on their faces as they brazenly posed their manhood by using profanity at an elevated volume in a docile, suburban one-stop junk shop.

Another sorry sign, of our sour times.

Searching

————

We're all looking for something; When our sights are set too low or we're always viewing the next bar as too high, we very well may never find it. When the search ends, development halts, and our true potential looks down on us and laughs, knowing there's no danger of us reaching it...

———————————————————

I played lacrosse when I was a kid. I liked it, I was pretty good at it, and it made my parents happy. When I was 11 I came across a BMX bike riding magazine at the grocery store, and long story short, everything else took a back seat to the compulsion I had to find out as much as I could about this unique *(and at the time, bizarre and unconventional)* culture. The imagery was brash and bold, the players in the *"game"* were wild and looked like people you might be afraid of if you saw them walking in your neighborhood; I couldn't get enough. The idea of *"convention",* while I probably didn't define it as such at 11 or 12 years old, changed immediately for me. The stability and simplicity of team sports *(and the just-add-water social circle they often create)* stepped aside to make way for a path that didn't make sense to anyone but me...

All of a sudden I wanted to explore, and experiment, and do so on my own. I saved up for a suitable bike and had an older neighborhood kid modify my current one so I could jump it off the ramp we made; In all its simplicity, I knew even then that I had opened an un-closable door. I had found direction and a sense of purpose based on organic personal interest, not traditional paint-by-numbers.

Soon after and through similar channels, I found hardcore music.

The imagery was just as brash, the cast of characters was even MORE menacing and intriguing, I couldn't have been further out of my element- But that just made me more curious and driven to seek. I went and found it, and it was just as scary and wild and exciting as I had envisioned.

I took buses, walked, rode my bike, snuck, schemed, and struggled to see and hear as much music as I could. The music was great, but the culture, and the way the interactions went between the participants- I was enthralled. There were fights, and riots, and lectures, and literature, and thought... and somehow the entire paradox just worked.

I had now found the two things that would shape my entire outlook, influence my life, and ultimately create my career path... and I was just barely a teenager.

The more I learned, the more I wanted to learn. I rode my bike constantly, I was as involved in the hardcore music scene as I could be while maintaining a normal high school schedule and suitable grades, and I was LEARNING.

I was *"learning"* at school, but in my *other* life I was learning how to interact in and adapt to any situation imaginable, use very limited resources to their full potential, never dismiss anything as TOO far, or TOO scary, or too much work... because ultimately, those would prove to be the things that meant the most, stuck with me, and taught lessons that I could never have learned without... doing them.

I feel lucky to have been exposed to independent culture and a critical thought process at an early age. Through BMX bike riding and hardcore I have owned and run companies, organized and executed world-class bike contests, booked huge shows with amazing bands, gotten paid to wear shoes, made money for some great people, written for magazines, been documented in photo and video, met and worked with many of my childhood idols... and for each of those *positive* things, there was a struggle, setback, or disappointment to match.

Learning about yourself, challenging convention, and *seeing* how far you can go instead of being TOLD how far you can go is never a simple path, but *"simple"* isn't really what most of us are searching for. We may have some self-deception in place that tells us what we want is a simple, basic life- and while elements of that may be true, ANY critical thinker, progressivist, subversionist, naysayer, questioner, or idealist knows that the simpler the journey, the less fulfilling the destination.

Even the most grounded and self-assured of us has a tendency to continue the search, and that self-awareness should never be ignored. FIND something, LEARN something, TRY something, and be open to the idea that even if you hate it, suck at it, or only try it once, the *searching* itself teaches the most valuable lesson.

Relying on fate or waiting for direction from the universe is most often a recipe for disappointment and unrealized potential; You will only be given a *fraction* of what you have the power to *take*.

Empowerment, development, and *realized* potential come from within; When the path to their achievement goes dark, the only way to find it again is to *look harder...*

"A man who wants to lead the orchestra must turn his back on the crowd." *James Crook*

POPCORN!

At least some of my post-work time each day is spent practicing social assimilation... Attempting to appear comfortable in whatever surroundings I'm in while not letting on that I am very often anything but. It's kind of a fun game for a while, though no matter how good I've gotten at it, after a few decades it just makes you feel like a fucking freak.

For quite a while now, 2nd Street in Long Beach, California has provided many of those surroundings. The east 2nd Street area has somehow remained clean and docile even though many neighboring it have gone the very opposite direction. Some of the older shops have been pushed aside, as is the way, but enough have remained that the area has avoided the *"shopping mall"* feel.

One of the strangest business marriages I've ever seen is the small, upscale gym located directly in the center of the shopping strip, and the large Irish pub located directly above. There is an indoor stairway from one to the other, large plexi-glass windows overlooking portions of the gym from the feeding trough upstairs, and- in case you need to get some deep-fried zucchini and a few beers right after exercising but forgot your wallet- your gym membership card can be used to charge food and drink. Maybe it only seems strange to me, but it is definitely curious to watch people finish with one and transition directly to the other. But as I've said before, they're almost certainly happier than I am, so who the fuck am I to criticize.

While offering no more cultural significance than a Polish sausage cart, the location of this particularly bland *"Irish Pub"* would allow it success even if it were called *'The Non-Elective Russian Roulette Club'...* Attractive crowd every night, upstairs outdoor patio- If I'm trying to improve at normal, that is where I needed to be. So, I went.

I had been there several times with a person or two and it had gone pretty well. Fun was had, no real trouble was caused, and each instance gave me a little boost of confidence that I was capable of existing in normal social situations. Tonight there was a notable sporting event playing, but it was early, so I easily found a seat and began the decision-making process. I opted for popcorn and water to start, and possibly a hard cider if I decided to really go all-out. The popcorn machine looked haggard and did not inspire confidence but I again defaulted to the masses, and if they can do it, so can I. I paid the bartender $1, was given my straw bowl lined with cheap bar napkins, and off I went.

There was soccer, boxing, and baseball playing on opposing TV's, and watching the very different reactions people had to each was an entertaining sport of its own. I ate my popcorn, slowly drank the hard cider I had opted for, and... relaxed. A couple people that recognized me in passing from the gym had said a quick hello, and there was even one female bartender that seemed to be extra glad I was there. I was enjoying myself, in spite of myself, and it felt good. I refilled my popcorn and water, wondered hard how people were able to watch an entire game of baseball, and thought even harder about how fast the one lightweight boxer was- even in comparison to his well-trained opponent- and how humbling it must be for those without that speed to work with him in training.

Having watched the first few Steven Segal movies far too many times growing up *(Above the Law, Out for Justice, Hard to Kill...)*, and also having been in more than an average amount of quirky indoor scuffles, there were a few things that always just looked like... fun. Stuff you never thought would happen, but in kind of an odd way romanticized- both due to its semi-fictional quality and just sheer spectacle.

I had finished my cider and gone to the restroom, and while returning to the table, noticed someone eating my popcorn. I could easily have been mistaken for having left the bar- water and popcorn half-full, cider empty. I was far from angry about it, and immediately upon reaching the table smiled and joked *"...well, now you owe me $.50!"* His two friends kind of laughed, and I sat back down, but the popcorn thief was not nearly as amused. He was obviously a little drunk, but still semi-present, and kind of stumbled over what to do next. He wanted to say something but couldn't quite settle on what, and instead just looked at me with his best hard-guy face and then backed away en route to his original seat. The way his friends immediately began navigating the situation told me that he was the hothead of the group. The girl put her hand on his back, and the guy kind of leaned over and whispered a few things to him, probably in an effort to calm him down and hopefully put the simple situation into its proper perspective.

I ate a few more pieces of popcorn and contemplated getting another drink, all the while holding a subtle but watchful eye over the nearby group. The popcorn thief was still very obviously unsettled, which was confusing and also totally stupid, since our interaction was one sentence long and my tone was not the slightest bit inflammatory. As he got up to go to the restroom and I looked over at his friends, they gave me their best shrugged-shoulder, hands up, half-eye-roll saying *"That's our crazy friend!"* I took that as both confirmation that they would not intervene if anything more serious occurred, and also that they were totally unequipped to deal with a drunk hothead. Considering all the factors, and knowing my luck, I decided to forgo another drink and begin my short walk home.

Distracted briefly by boxing while putting on my coat, the popcorn thief had made about half his way from the restroom before I noticed, and was headed towards *my* table, not his. I was truly shocked that it was even still being thought about, but at this point I was also cued-in and definitely not unprepared for whatever happened next. Now hovering near the table, he mumbled something about being disrespected in front of his friends; I responded with my opinion that I had not done so, and that the entire thing was a simple and kind of funny misunderstanding. He rattled off some dumb bar-guy stuff about *"me talking shit",* stepped backward, and at the same time began looking at the floor *(most people entering into a misguided confrontation are not confident enough in their stance to look someone square in the eye beforehand).* I said *"OK man, well I'm sorry you're upset."*

As soon as my sentence ended he lunged forward and attempted to shove me into the wall behind us. He got his hands on me and was strong, but so was I, and he was drunk. He lost his footing for a second, I got a good hold under an arm and on his belt... And as I had loved on screen but never thought I would get to do, tripped and threw him right into, onto, and over the table his friends were sitting at. The noise was kind of satisfying, his friends popped up and out of the way as if the floor had opened into lava, and the table itself rolled back and forth a little bit as it lay on its side on the ground. Some glasses had smashed, the popcorn thief had climbed clumsily *(and wet...)* back to his feet, and the bar security guard had joined us and was ready to mediate if necessary; I was again disappointed but not surprised at the outcome of a seemingly simple night and what should have been an innocuous situation.

I was asked to leave out of protocol, but having seen the unfolding, both the bartender and the guard said they knew the altercation wasn't my fault and I was welcome back any time. The same was not to be said of the popcorn thief. Now disrespected, wet, and kicked out of a bar I'm sure he intended to return to, hope could be had that when he dried out he would see how silly and unnecessary the short ordeal was. The 11% optimist in me likes to believe that a lesson may have been learned, but the remaining 89% realist ends up digesting the sour reality that very often, this is just how people are.

I also frequently wonder if I give off some type of pheromone or electric current that magnetizes assholes and disrespectful louts to me in the most precarious of times and manners; Luck is luck, but pattern is pattern, and I'm not sure where my scales balance, or why. I have settled on the fact that being engaged in my surroundings in an active way, and actually acknowledging the presence and proximity of others, is both a positive and a negative; I believe many appreciate the courtesy, and I end up speaking with some that I otherwise never would have, but others seem to find it inflammatory or confrontational.

The ones that take it the negative way are the same sort, I imagine, that blame their girlfriends when they get lost en route to the token day at the lake, or shove someone after an unintentional shoulder bump in a crowded bar... Or that have never met a consequence for an action, and still feel that they are above doing so. Denial, arrogance, discourtesy, hot-headedness... With the direction society is headed, the deadly sins list needs to be expanded to at least 15.

This unintentional sociology experiment ends with simple confirmation that sometimes assholes are just assholes, and no addition or subtraction of libation or situation is going to change it. The misguided, soft-bodied man's-man that shoved me would very likely have done the same thing had I accidentally dripped ice cream on one of his fucking boat shoes at a child's birthday party; When insecurity and weakness live that close to the surface, it doesn't take much to draw them out.

The end finds me thankful that I can *(at least most of the time)* internalize and... perspectivize... my insecurities- not drench those around me with them as if they'd volunteered to be mixed in the drink.

HELL ON EARTH

PRESENTS

9 SHOCKS TERROR

DEVOID OF FAITH

SHODOKAN

BREAK OF DAWN

VERTEX - Liberty Pole Way, Rochester NY
Saturday August 1st   5 PM $6
CALL HELL FOR MORE INFORMATION

(The beginning, 1995)

(Steve Crandall, Bob Rathbun, Greg Walsh, 2001)

First Ever
HELL ON EARTH
Warehouse Sale
Great deals on all kinds of gear, limited edition stuff, and bands...

FACE VALUE
The return of Cleveland's prodigal son's of bitches!
Ex- 9 Shocks Terror, H-100's

★DEATH THREAT★
You can laugh and talk behind my back, it only fuels my fire.

CROWNS OF KINGS
CT Hardcore. New on Reaper Records

with special guests

Dawn of War

Like Wolves

Sunday August 10th, 2008.
All Ages. $8.00 at the door
3:00 pm doors and shopping. 4:30 Bands

315 Alexander Street. Rochester, New York 14607

---

info: 585-288-6830. myspace.com/hellonearthstore

RUSTBELT  *Coalition*

(Photo by Ben Pritchard (RIP), 2005)

Greg Walsh

(Wolf Brigade, War of Attrition , Hell on Earth)

selling, signing
(and possibly reading from)
new novel
Theft of the Age

BARNES&NOBLE

at College Town
1305 Mount Hope Ave.
Rochester, NY 14620

Sunday, November 6th, 2016
1pm-3pm

(There will be swear words, descriptions of
violence, as well as discussion of disturbing
concepts such as the use of discretion and
common sense: Attend with caution.)

www.wolfbrigade.com
www.warofattrition.com

Theft of the Age

Greg Walsh

(Photo by Steve Crandell, 2

HELL ON EARTH

presents

LA REVOLUTION

SEPT. 27th & 28th 2003

PRIMO

X-DREAMS SKATEPARK

3195 Brighton-Henrietta Townline Rd
Rochester, NY 14623
585-424-6510
www.xdreamspark.com

fbm bike company

$5.00 spectate **$50. am $80. pro**
40 rider limit each class - pre-register or get there early!
registration starts at 9:00 am, doors at 10:00 am
am event and pro practice saturday, pro event sunday.

additional info and registration: hell on earth- 585-232-1560 or
www.hellonearthstore.com

BRIDGE NINE

Fender

(The Abyss, 1994)

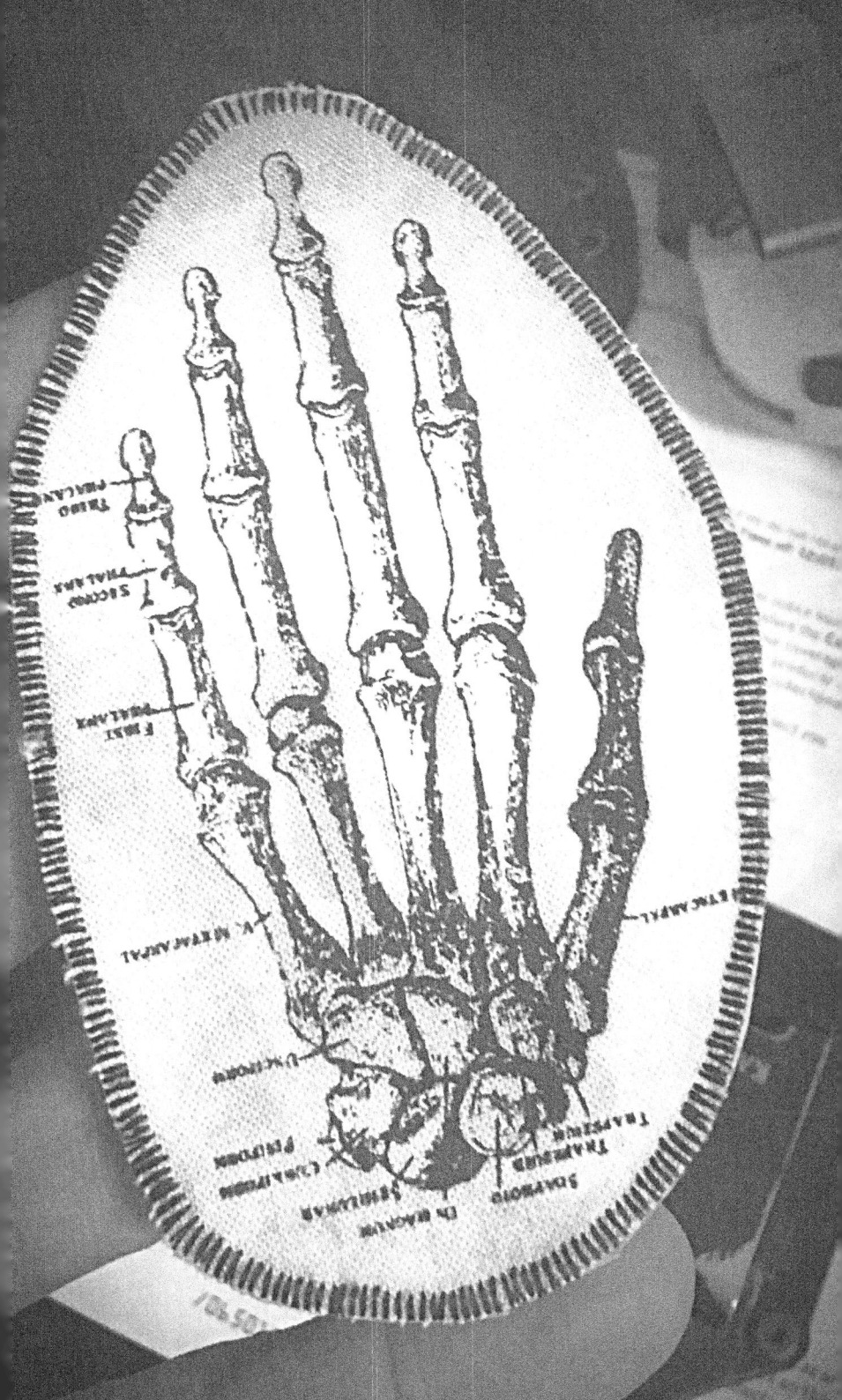

"He ain't heavy, Father..he's m' brother"

DRINKING GAMES

When I selected my shirt for the evening I'm quite sure I put consideration into the reaction it might evoke- I was likely hoping for curiosity, questioning, and maybe even a bit of intimidation. The music I had gotten into over the past few years made me feel those things in spades, and I misguidedly assumed that anyone in my eventual surroundings would share them. The shirt was either from the band Suicidal Tendencies or Overkill, and whichever one it was, the imagery and language were kind of severe; I was 15, and neck-deep in a somewhat frightening underground scene that I thought was the coolest thing in the world, partially for those very reasons.

We had gone to Buffalo to visit our aunt, uncle, and cousins, and for me that meant sneakily watching rated "R" movies that I probably would not have gotten to see otherwise, shoplifting prolifically with my cousin at the local mall, or attempting to matriculate with his somewhat uppity social circle. I stood out in demeanor *(as well as appearance)* at such gatherings however my general pleasantness had always allowed for nice conversations with a few of the girls that tended to be around. The party this time around was at the house of a well-to-do boy whose parents were out of town... cliché, yes, but that is what kids did in the world I was visiting. It seemed like a merry-go-round of traveling social events based on adult absence and availability of cheap alcohol. I didn't get it, and it in no way resembled my life in Rochester, but I was there and decided to ride the ride.

The yard was crowded even as we arrived, and there were very few people I recognized. The house itself was beautiful, and I remember thinking what a chore it would be to restore it to its pre-teenage wasteland state, though I'm sure the young proprietors had plenty of experience in executing post-party makeovers.

I wandered through the house, into the backyard, and eventually down into the lavishly furnished and accessorized basement. There was an ordinary-ness to it all, even in its pomp and frills; The most beautiful things very often require the least effort to be so, and the forcefulness of the grandeur cheapened the appeal. There were small clusters of kids in all rooms, and among them were just three I had met before- all girls, and all appearing quite popular.

My cousin had disappeared just a few minutes after our arrival, and while sitting by myself on a basement couch watching MTV on the large-for-the-time television, I rationalized that having a beer might make the ordeal feel a little more normal. It would be my first drink of alcohol, and although I was not without reservation about it, I settled on a *"What's the harm?"* perspective and went about it. It was in a can- *Budweiser*- and it was disgusting. In addition to tasting terrible I'm quite sure it was supposed to be much colder- I wasn't drinking for enjoyment nearly as much as fuel for social integration, so taste be damned.

Feeling less like an outcast now that I was flying the same flag as most of the others, I wandered around a bit and said hello to the three girls I had previously met. Two were engaged in some very theatrical gossip/ storytelling and didn't have the time of day, and the third- Kirsten- seemed happy to talk to someone outside her usual circle. We talked about school, we laughed a little bit about how similar everyone looked and acted, and I asked her what she did outside of school for enjoyment. She said *"Oh, just normal things. Parties, the mall, I played soccer in 9th grade but got cut in 10th so now I just play tennis with my mom and her friends."* None of that struck me as normal, but then again, if I had told her that I routinely snuck out of my house and traveled hundreds of miles to see shows that often ended in violence and mayhem, and almost daily threw myself down stairs on a bicycle for fun, I'm sure she would have felt the same.

I finished my first beer and Kirsten had gotten me a second which I began drinking as we talked. I wasn't drunk, but *was* fuzzy, and between beer and conversation none of my attention was focused elsewhere. At this point she and I were talking about our few pieces of common ground, including curiosity as to how anyone could actually *like* math, and the recent shocking discovery that one of the stars of *'Beverly Hills, 90210* was actually in her *thirties.*

I remember feeling unusual, but also slightly normal, and impressed with my effort to blend. I heard some commotion behind me and upon seeing a strange look come across Kirsten's face, I turned towards it just in time for mine to be struck with what appeared to be a small metal folding chair. I fell, was again struck by several boys upon attempting to rise, and then grabbed and brought outside. I was dizzy from both alcohol and blows to the head, and was relatively defenseless against the group that had now put me in what was presumably their parents van. They seemed older than I, and their taunting told me that I had been targeted based simply on the fact that I had the nerve to talk to a girl they knew, and that I looked like a *"freak"*. *(In reflection, I am sure that I stood out, but the freaks I pictured were always those with prominent piercings, colored hair, elaborate ornamentation on their clothing and jackets... I simply had Vans shoes, Dickies pants, and a music*

T-shirt. Strange to think how drastically times have changed in that regard.)

I was attempting to shield myself in a back corner of the van, definitely not knowing the endgame or what else I could have done to improve my situation. I had been hit multiple times in the stomach and sides, at least that many in the head, and was in a lot of pain. My hand was bleeding a little bit, so I thought, but I later realized it had trickled down from my nose. I attempted to shift while continuing to cover my head and face, and as what would be the last round of taunting began one of the boys kicked me high in the chest, snapping my head back and splitting it open on the rear door of the van. The warm liquid trickling down my neck brought me to anger, but it was overwhelmed and quieted by pain and fear. I had gone out briefly at that point, and awoke to the doors being opened and then being put down on a sidewalk in what looked to be an industrial part of town. The short time after was a blur, and the next clarity I had was climbing to my feet and beginning to walk.

It had gotten colder and was well past dusk. I had no idea where I was, and the frustration I felt for getting myself into such a situation now rivaled the pain driving through my body and head. Upon coming to a cross street I opted to stay in one place, assuming that if Buffalo were anything like Rochester there would soon be a cop, or a bus, or at least a group of students that may be able to direct me to a phone or store. After waiting for what felt like hours, but was surely less than ten minutes, a cop drove by and I flagged him down with my arms. I briefly described what had transpired, including the fact that I had drank one and a half cans of beer at a party and that I could give neither the full name of anyone in attendance or the address, and then provided my uncle's name. After patting me down and threatening to ticket me for vagrancy, he put me in the back of the car and drove to the police station.

The third time in the back of a police car was certainly less of a rush than the first two- one of which was for riding my bike on private property in the city of Rochester, and the other was simply for standing in the wrong place at the wrong time as violence escalated quickly in front of a show venue. I was fortunate enough not to get into any trouble in either of the previous back seat visits, but distinctly remembered a feeling of excitement and a small sense of wonder accompanying each. This time, however, I felt angry to be there- based both on the disturbing nature of its origin, and the fact that I was casually accused of something *(albeit as minor as vagrancy...)* while visibly injured and scared. My now head-to-toe shaking was surely caused by a combination of temperature, pain, and anger, and was severe enough to make me dizzy as I stared at the computerized screen in the front of the car.

I was led into the station and pointed to a chair as the officer that drove me in spoke with another and then picked up a phone. I could overhear enough to know that he had called my uncle, and that *he* would immediately be on his way. My heart sank a bit further with the thought of him telling my parents what had transpired, and I was already picturing the lot of them coming into the station and chastising me for all manners of the irresponsibility I had exhibited that evening. I watched the goings-on of the station and attempted to eavesdrop anywhere I could, mostly in an effort to distract myself from what was now severe pain in my ribs, back, and head. Before long my uncle arrived, alone, and after blowing by the front desk walked briskly towards my escorting officer. My uncle was a thick, jovial, big-hearted man, and in all his jolly charm and good humor, he was also a bit of an imposing figure. A local waste management magnate, he had obviously been through the ringer many times and had developed the take-no-shit attitude that came with.

The officer began explaining his version of what had transpired, but after taking one look at me, my uncle went up one side of him and down the other for the fact that I was not already being looked at in the hospital and instead sitting unattended in a bloody t-shirt alongside criminals waiting for booking. He was livid, and frightening, and since I had not done anything punishable and was obviously pretty banged up, the officer conceded *(but not before commenting that I hadn't stated I was injured)* and walked away. My uncle helped me up, put his hand on my back, and took me to the hospital.

On the way over, we talked about the version of the story that made sense to share, and settled on a simple one that involved some drunken boys picking on the out-of-towner and it getting a little out of hand. Though he knew full well what transpired at parties such as the one we had attended, he also knew that telling my parents served no purpose other than to further upset everyone involved. After leaving the station and now learning that I would likely not be getting grounded for the rest of my young adult life, the pain quieted to a dull roar.

We arrived at the hospital and were checked in quickly. The experience was unremarkable and thankfully efficient, and taught us that I had a mild concussion, required nine stitches in the back of my head, and had at least two bruised ribs. I was cared for, wrapped up, and sent on our way.

Upon returning to my uncles' house, I was beyond thankful to see all but one light turned off. I moved quietly, knowing that a shower and some sleep would lessen the visual impact on my parents, and though I'm sure they were awake and waiting for us to return, I was so exhausted that trying to explain myself right then might have done me in. Sleep was welcome but not comfortable, and the thought of what had transpired that night left me feeling strong relief that it hadn't been any worse. My parents and the others in the house were understandably concerned when we convened over breakfast in the morning, but my uncle did a masterful job at downplaying the entire thing and minimizing the elements of the story that would have caused the most commotion. It hurt to breathe, and my head was throbbing like a rung bell, but I was able to conceal at least enough of it keep the house from entering a full-blown red alert.

We spent a low-key half day lounging in- and out- of doors, and then headed back to Rochester in the early evening. I had quickly filled my cousin in on what had transpired, and he was both furious and profoundly apologetic. I just wanted to get back to my version of reality *(in which I couldn't be the weirdest one in the room if I tried)* and use this as a lesson and example of paths I would never walk again. Experiencing the fear of helplessness, and of knowing that even my best efforts wouldn't have unwound the tangle I was in, became weights I carried that didn't lighten until I made deliberate efforts to ensure they would never happen again.

In the cycle of over-thinking I had done in the years following this event, it wasn't until I examined it with wide-eyes and pragmatism that the positive benefit and truth were found. My one-day foray into the herd mentality of teenage drinking and directionless socialization taught me a swift, harsh lesson- but the less-harsh, more gradual lesson that befell many of my schoolmates is arguably much more severe...

Many kids my age found such allure in the pastimes and circumstances that I visited and tried to assimilate in that they *became* them.

They drank and partied and social-climbed their way right through high school, likely into college, and some probably even made it work for them beyond that. But a strong argument could be made that they would have been better in at least some aspect of their lives had they not as young adults been so consumed with consumption and addicted to attention.

There is a strength in solitude and a clarity in defiance that I had now begun to understand, but that can't be explained and must be experienced...

A misadventure such as this *(even with its costly scars)* was necessary, and taught an invaluable lesson that would have been impossible to grasp without being forced to feel.

the WARM LIQUID trickling down my neck brought me to ANGER but it was quickly OVERWHELMED and QUIETED by PAIN and

SUICIDAL TENDENCIES

FEAR

DEAD DOG #1

At 14, I had already begun to feel like an outcast in both my personal and professional lives. My *"professional"* life was school, of course, and having recently turned the corner from matriculating lacrosse player into alienating BMX bike rider, it felt like I had disaligned with the prominent, acceptable political party. At the time, the two worlds did not cleanly overlap, and all but a few of my friends from one ran for the hills when I began to prioritize the other.

One carry-over was a popular kid, a sports standout, and the son of the football coach. He was a lifer in the conventional system, but had an affinity for the fringes where I now resided. He rode BMX with me whenever he could, and was good at it, and in my opinion him doing so was one of the only reasons that I wasn't even more severely ostracized.

We got along well- causing trouble wherever we could find it, listening to Suicidal Tendencies on near-constant repeat, and riding bikes like we were being paid to do so. Being a sports kid in a sports family, I believed that things like football and lacrosse must have felt almost like jobs to him, and bike riding *(especially with me)* must have felt like a nearly-supreme rebellion.

Most nights I would pedal my bike home, even though it was quite a trek from our usual riding spots to my parents' house outside of town, but I usually didn't mind the process and enjoyed the independence. It had gotten especially late one evening, and at our last stop I had gotten a flat tire. Not an unusual occurrence by any means, but the bike shop was closed and we had no other means to fix it. The ride was taxing but manageable, but the walk would have been a little much.

My parents were MIA *(or maybe the phone line was busy)* so the last resort became asking his dad to drive me. A burly, stern sports-guy, he had little patience for someone like me, and was not discreet or unclear about his lack of interest in shuttling me around. Moments after he begrudgingly agreed to do so, we carefully piled my bike into the trunk of his large sedan and made our way.

He was driving as if speed would erase the inconvenience he was feeling, and both his son and I felt the tension. Neither of us said a word, and the glances we shot back and forth were not accompanied by their usual smirks and smarm. Once we were outside town and had entered the rural area approaching where I lived, he sped up even a little further, and I remember it making me uncomfortable.

There was a cut-over street that contained a very old single-lane bridge, and upon crossing it we were then only a few miles from home. We were now relatively rural, and if my dad had conveyed anything to me during his driving lectures it was that it was better to be patient than sorry when driving on dark country roads. We were going way too fast, and the universe chose to let us know in a terrible way.

Like it had come from nowhere, a tall black dog was standing directly in the middle of the road, and nothing short of divine intervention could have kept us from hitting it. To this day, I believe it to have been a greyhound- black, with brown on its neck and paws. The speed at which we hit it essentially demolished the dog, and sent pieces flying a nearly surreal distance from the car. The noise and smell were sickening and washed over me in slow-motion, and I both covered and closed my eyes once I realized what had happened. The volume and ferocity of swearing from the adult in the front seat was shocking, and his anger quickly became directed at his son, and at me.

We pulled off the road and got out of the car to survey the damage. There was a large dent and a broken headlight on the left side of the car, but that seemed secondary to the mess that we now stood amongst. It appeared for a second that he was prepared to get back in the car and drive away, but reconsidered... kind of.

He conveyed that we needed to attempt to let the owners know what had happened, and I learned quickly that by *"we"*, he meant *"me"*. I felt truly awful for every aspect of what had unfolded- beginning with the cardinal sin of imposing on him for a ride- and the idea of having to tell someone that we had just killed their dog nearly made me cry. He sent me up to the nearest house as he stayed back by the car; It was in that moment that I lost all reverence for the outward appearance of men. Kind of a blessing, I suppose.

I knocked on the door, discovered that I had indeed found the owners, and pitifully conveyed my message of death. After doing so *(and having to stand there awash in its effect)*, I turned and walked back towards the still-running car, now a full handful of years older than I had been just a few hours prior.

DEAD DOG #2

When I was younger I had a few strange episodes that the doctors called *"Complex Partial Seizures"*. They would cause me to black out for a few moments, and for a short while after waking up, things were kind of blurry. Immediately prior to the blackout, I would see a strange picture in my mind, or flash back quickly to something from my past. Falling down the stairs of a hotel I was staying in with my parents and brother is what allowed them to learn I had been having them; I hadn't shared the information because I was approaching 16 and knew that they would *(justifiably)* never give a driver's license to someone that randomly went to sleep for a minute.

I was made to wait another year and a few months, which meant that I would be a little over 17 when I got my license. I'd had one or two more blackouts in the time since falling down the stairs, but didn't tell anyone because I was restless and felt I simply had to move my life forward. I had already been traveling extensively for both music and BMX bike riding, but I wanted to be able to do so independently and was unwilling to wait any longer.

Next door to my parents' house lived the Capanna's- an older couple that were both very private and very nice- and their dog named Bear. Mr. Capanna would play with and walk and sit on the porch with that dog for what seemed like all day, every day. Bear was nice, but very protective- not only of the older couple, but of the kids in the neighboring houses and very much so of my brother and I, since we were the closest and would play with and bring him treats when given permission.

A short time after I had gotten my license I had a serious argument with my parents, likely over the fact that I was not yet graduated from high school, and was already planning on moving to the city. I had also come home with blood on me at some ridiculous hour of the night before, and had also recently left town for two days to watch hardcore out of state. I wasn't your run-of-the-mill *"bad kid"*, but I was certainly a challenge.

I was stressed and angry, and in a hurry to leave. As I sat down in the car I remember feeling unspecifically *"off"*, but decided to go anyway and address it on the road. As soon as I started the car and began to move in reverse, I blacked out. Even though I was always given a tiny warning, it was seldom early enough to do anything about what came next, and the same was true here.

The car rolled backwards down the curved driveway and ended up in the lawn, and in the process, hit Bear. I hadn't even seen him near the car, due to my haste and self-involvement, and he was likely walking towards it to say hello when I started backing up. I was dizzy from the blackout, but aware of what I had done. He wasn't dead, but he wasn't OK. It was obvious that he was not going to get up and walk it off, and for the first and only time in my entire life, I took the weak way out and drove off.

I couldn't handle the idea of my carelessness ruining something that brought enjoyment to such nice people, or that I had hurt something that had done nothing but protect me. I also flashed back to a few-years-prior incident in which I was the bearer of similar bad news and it shook me for quite some time; In a moment of un-clarity, the emotional gravity of conveying the information managed to outweigh the right-minded notion to do so.

I went to a friend's house and waited. He wasn't home, but I had a key, so I just sat there sobbing. My parents knew where I was going, so I knew that shortly there would be a call telling me what had happened. When it came I lied to them and said that I had seen Bear as I was leaving the house but had no idea I had hit him. They told me Mr. Capanna had taken him to the vet, but that it didn't look good. Bear died, and I believe that day when I was 17 was the last time I ever felt like a good person.

My parents didn't push me on the particulars of the situation, though I partially wish they would have. I have always thought they had an inkling that I had blacked out, but just never mentioned it. After it was all over, I went and apologized to Mr. Capanna; He was very gracious in accepting it, but there was very little contact between us after. I did everything I could to help them whenever I was at my parent's house- shovel, pick things up, etc., but no amount of trivial yard chores could ever un-do how I felt about what happened, and even more so the cowardly manner in which I handled it.

I'm sitting here crying a little bit as I re-visit this, and at this point it was a LONG time ago; I've had some pretty fucked up things happen that have played big parts in defining my character, but this may be the only one that I did completely to myself, and am 100% to blame for the outcome.

I've thought about this situation thoroughly and often... It serves as a reminder that there is never an excuse to be careless or selfish when such actions have even the slightest potential to damage someone else. I hurt that old man because I was so caught up in anger and haste that I was paying no attention to anything else.

This situation *(and a few others in the same vein)*, is why my patience is virtually infinite with those close to me, but nearly non-existent with myself.

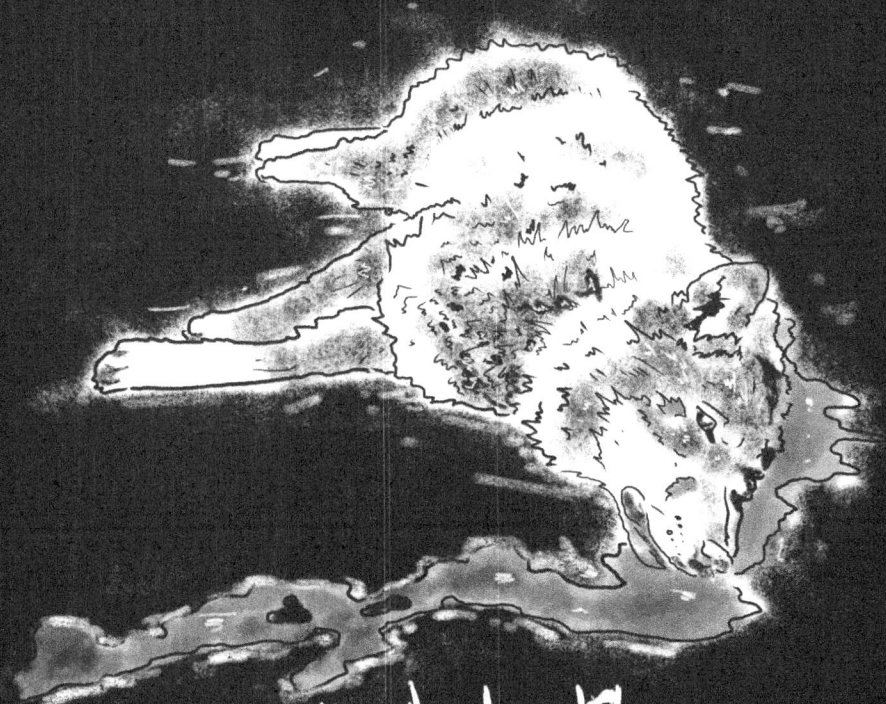

"that day when I was 17
was the last time I ever felt
like a GOOD PERSON..."

THINGS I'VE STOLEN, PART ONE

I don't consider myself a person who steals, necessarily; Certainly not a thief. But I have stolen a handful of non-basic items each from equally unusual locations, and if presented with the option of a do-over, would handle at least a few of the situations differently.

In no particular order of vulgarity or priority:

#1: *Hedgehog from a pet store in Eastview Mall*

(Re-handling: *Same.*)

I worked at the mall for a period of time as a teenager, and while doing so made friends with an interesting girl that worked at the nearby music store *(once upon a time there were these cool little retailers that sold almost nothing but music and assorted music-related novelties)*. She was unusual and, if for no other reason, we got along because neither of us felt any more at home in our weird work settings than we did in our own skin, but we were both really good at pretending in... both.

As we got to know each other and began to rely on the commiseration during our overlapping workdays, no stone was left unturned when it came to addressing things we disliked about the mall, or that which we loved outside of it. One particular conversation uncovered that she had always wanted a hedgehog, and that she found it especially hard to go near the awful pet store at the entrance of the mall because as one of the smaller, oversight-types of pets, they were treated and maintained horribly.

Mall pet stores, even at their very best, are terrible and damnable- and this one was far from a shining example of the species. Not long after our conversation I began investigating, and though until that point I'm quite sure I had never seen one in person, I decided I was going to liberate one of those poor captive pincushions and give it to her as a gift.

The idea of simply buying one had crossed my mind, but as a part-time mall health food store employee, $65 for a spiked hamster might as well have been $650... and there was no theatre in paying for something they shouldn't have been selling anyway. I concocted a thorough- albeit risky- plan and presented it to my intended accomplices.

It was a four-person scheme: The out-of-store diversion, the in-store distraction, the mid-store watchdog, and the hands-on liberator. As it was my idea, I elected to take the risk, and intended to stuff the prickly little rodent into a Gap bag that had been pre-filled with clothes, towels, and newspaper. The hands-on part of the plan very simply involved me reaching into the cage, grabbing the hedgehog, putting it in the bag, and then casually walking out of the store.

Here are a few things I had not considered/ known prior to the liberation:

- Hedgehogs are surprisingly sharp when they are mad, and extremely difficult to grab quickly and quietly, even though I kept telling it that this is for its own good.

- When removed from their familiar environment, hedgehogs freak out like one of those idiotic hippies on drugs at a terrible outdoor festival. That little sucker was bouncing around in the bag like it was on fire and had a bee in its shorts.

- Hedgehogs also make a loud tick/ chirp when alarmed, and I was sure that if the sight of the Mexican jumping bean running wall-to-wall in the used Gap bag didn't draw attention, the noise certainly would.

The others had excelled in their roles. Accomplice #1 knocked over a garbage can in the main mall, and then began shouting and carrying on as if possessed... The sole pet store employee watched attentively, as we had hoped, and the in-store distraction began talking to him in an effort to keep him there. The watchdog gave me the signal, and I then began the most ham-fisted theft of a hedgehog ever to go on record.

Somehow, between the screaming kid with an afro in the main mall, the bizarre conversation initiated by accomplice #2, and my uncanny ability to act normal when things are anything but, I managed to walk out past the employee with a gyrating, clicking, and now blood-covered Gap bag containing a hedgehog that would be given as a gift that very same day, and in the very same wrapping paper. He was appreciated completely *(especially when accompanied by the story of his escape)*, given the name Elliot, and lived happily for nearly a decade after his sketchy but successful release from captivity.

#2: *TV from Sears in the Buffalo mall*

(Re-handling: *Same.*)

My cousin and I had a love/ hate relationship as teenagers. We both liked to circumvent rules and challenge things that seemed better left alone, but with very different motivations and with very different goals in mind. I didn't trust him as far as I could throw him, and justifiably so, but we partnered-in-crime when the opportunity arose because we had complimentary underhanded strengths. Basically, it was a mischief-oriented circle of snakes that very often led to near-brushes with trouble larger than either of us probably realized at the time.

After causing some trouble, getting away with it, and knowing it was time to leave, we noticed a strange sign in front of the electronics department in the Sears store we were cutting through on our way out of the mall. The look we gave each other as we stopped and stared certainly may have resembled one staged in a movie or sitcom- confused but curious, pleased but suspicious... What we had come upon was a sign stating *"Please excuse our dust- we're renovating our security system."*

Nearly unbelievable, still to this day, but there it sat... baiting us to see what it really meant. The only logical thing to do was walk a few laps of the store to evaluate staffing and exit strategies, and then find something suitably unreasonable to attempt to walk out with. Confidence is a big part of successfully taking anything that isn't yours, and we wanted to insulate ours by not simply relying on their thick-headedness; We performed our due diligence, continued to shake our heads in confusion as to the giant *"Steal from us"* sign they had put up in arguably the most expensive section of their store, and then began the selection process.

We decided based both on youthful exuberance and misguided confidence to attempt to lift up and take out a large, flat-screen TV. Flat-screen TV's were very new at the time, and the one we had our eyes on was not cheap. My cousin knew that his friend was moving into a new apartment that very week, and was sure we could get at least half of the retail price from him in cash; If it worked, it would be more money than I ever had at one time. A quick trip to a payphone in the main portion of the mall confirmed it, and all of a sudden we had both a timeline and a buyer for our highly questionable, yet-to-be-attempted plan.

For some reason in our heightened state cookies seemed like the best use of our time. After sharing and inhaling a bag of what contained probably 30 tiny chocolate chip cookies *(they came 12 or 24 to a bag, but the girl at the cookie store seemed to like us...)*, we decided that the idea wasn't going to get any better, and to just get on with it.

The plan was simple: Walk into the electronics section and look around a bit, act as if we're waiting for someone, say hello to at least one of the employees working the area, and then pick up the large box containing the TV and walk out the double doors located not 50 feet from the sign that birthed the entire idea.

We needed to keep our heads up, walk slowly, and even voluntarily set the box down and joke with each other once during the trip; Teenagers in the midst of stealing a giant television, we thought, wouldn't be patient with the process of removing it from the store. Who knows if it worked, but giving any onlookers the feeling that we weren't stealing seemed like an important consideration.

I was walking backwards and he was walking forwards, and so I got the final view into the electronics section and the adjoining aisles of the store. No one even really looked at us-people's eyes passed over, but none set, and the mixed feeling as my back hit the exit door was one of relief and confusion. We weren't out of the woods yet, but once we crossed the threshold the chance of anyone coming for us dropped exponentially. Once we cleared the doors we walked to the nearest loading dock and placed the box on the adjacent curb.

For as potentially disastrous as a situation like that could have been, the finale was about as uneventful as it could have been; My cousin's friend showed up on time, we loaded the box into the back seat of his car, and he paid us in cash... We ended up with $325 each, and at the time that might as well have been $3,000.

We collected ourselves, made our way to the front of the mall, and called my aunt from a payphone to come pick us up.

Like nothing had ever happened.

#3: *'Welcome to Vermont' sign*

(Re-handling: *Different. Fuck that.*)

Anyone that has traveled extensively by car knows that breaking monotony *(even alongside the bizarre cast of characters I've been fortunate enough to run around with)* gets harder as time goes on. Some people listen to audio books, some people sing to themselves... we would often choose to make a sport of taking something during our journey and passing it on as a gift to someone when we arrived at our destination. It was mostly simple things: Weird posters and displays from rest stops, traffic cones with city markings, an occasional holiday decoration...

Oh, and one time, the giant metal *'Welcome to Vermont'* sign.

We would frequently overestimate our navigational abilities and underestimate time and distance, and end up with abnormal amounts of ground to cover in troublingly short amounts of time. In this particular instance, we were on our way from Rochester, NY to Middlebury, VT to pick up the kid that played bass in our band and drive him back to Rochester to make a record. The recording was to happen over the course of one weekend, and he didn't get out of class in Vermont until 6pm on Friday; The only thing that made any sense was to give him some time to have dinner, pick him up around 10pm, drive straight back to NY, put a whole record together in 48 hours, and then deliver him back.

When the time vs. distance ratio made little-to-no-sense, but the destination was important enough to roll the dice, there was only one driver I trusted. Our friend Curly was a perpetual-motion troublemaker, and also as good-natured and reliable as it got. While in high school, our band would frequently commit to out-of-town shows as far away as Cleveland or even once or twice Michigan, and his relentless commitment to both fun and trouble was the only thing that got me there and back between last bell in the afternoon and first bell the next morning.

The drive to Vermont was beautiful, and we had excellent hardcore from both NY and Cleveland and plenty of *Little Debbie chocolate peanut butter 'Nutty Bars'* to help us keep the pace. Our hustle limited our hands-on sightseeing, and by the time we neared Vermont, we were a little antsy and our gift basket was empty.

Conversation turned to what we might give away at an upcoming show of ours that looked like it might be a big one. Neither the show nor the giveaway were anything that anyone was losing sleep over or biting their nails in anticipation of, but that never mattered to us. We handled each and every one as if it were the most important, because to us- and possibly even just one other person- it was.

Having made it from Rochester without needing to break for gas, we stopped at a small store not far from the state line to refuel, get a snack, and stretch our legs. At some point during the pit stop we both looked up the road and noticed that there was a tall cover of grass surrounding the *'Welcome to...'* sign, and the wheels started turning. It was dark by then, and what had started with a little joking and laughter had now turned into us looking for a secluded place to park within short distance of the potential target.

We hustled from the parking spot to underneath the sign during a break in traffic and evaluated the situation. It was secured to the frame with six bolts, appeared to be roughly the footprint of the backseat and trunk of the car, and made it a point to tell us that it was due for a vacation and had been looking forward to doing some traveling.

As usual, we had both a wrench and a blanket, and one began the extraction process while the other watched vigilantly for cars and/ or foot traffic. Two weird-looking New Yorkers abducting the welcome mat to the hippie capital of the eastern United States would likely not have gone over too well, and with the car more than a stone's throw away, we weren't in an ideal flight position.

We had alternated between bolt removing and watching, and were down to #6. As was often the case with bike repairs, or music gear repairs, or anything of that nature, the last thing you want is usually what you get: The final bolt was not moving, and we were way too deep in the process to turn back now. The sign was hanging crooked and forward, and we had been working on it for nearly an hour. The only other tool we had at our disposal was a tire iron, and so as last resort, we decided to try to smash it free; Thankfully it worked. Un-rusted, we would likely have been out of luck, but it appeared no one had taken the sign down in a while.

When the bolt broke, the sign fell, and we quickly draped the blanket over it and ran as fast as two kids carrying a dinner-table-sized piece of wiggly aluminum could run. It fit in the car, luckily and barely, and as soon as the trunk closed we got the hell out of there and finished the first leg of our ridiculous weekend journey.

The sign ended up spending the weekend in a dorm room of the fancy college, much to the chagrin of one of the occupants, and then made its way home with us en route to becoming one of our most memorable, and certainly our riskiest, giveaways.

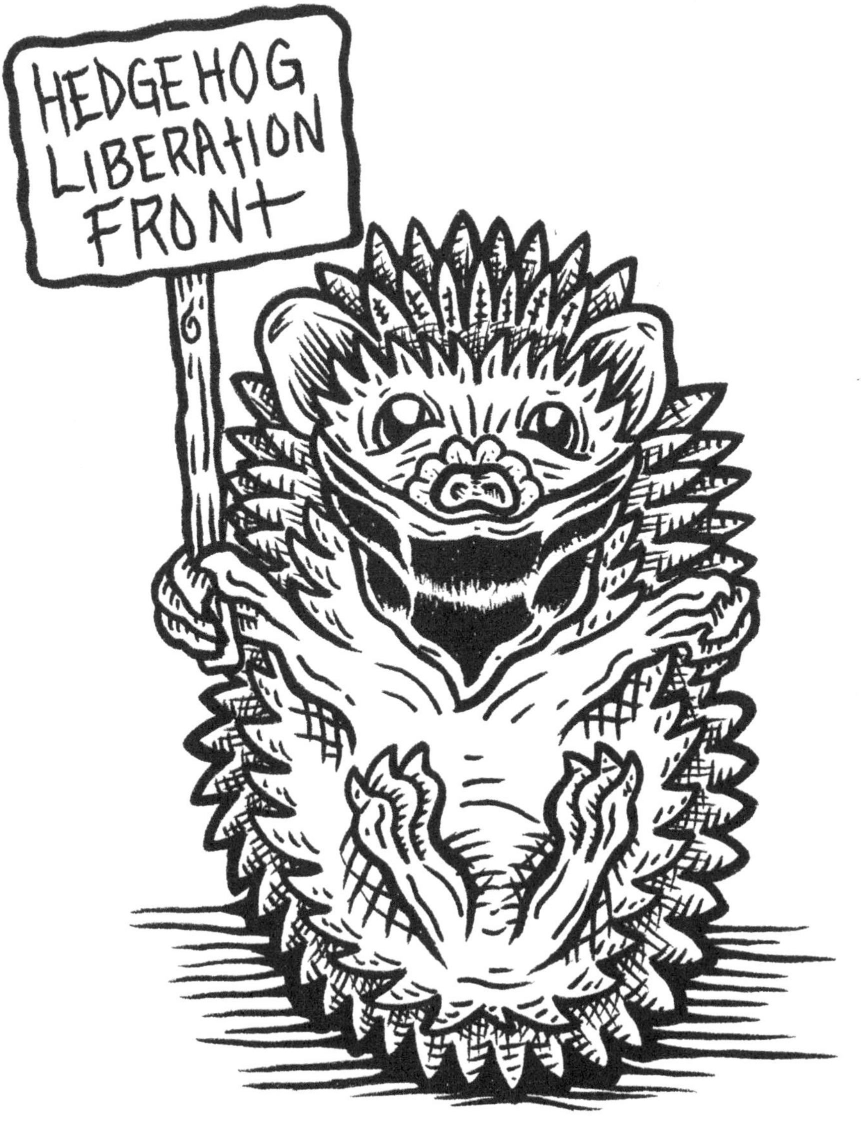
HEDGEHOG
LIBERATION
FRONT

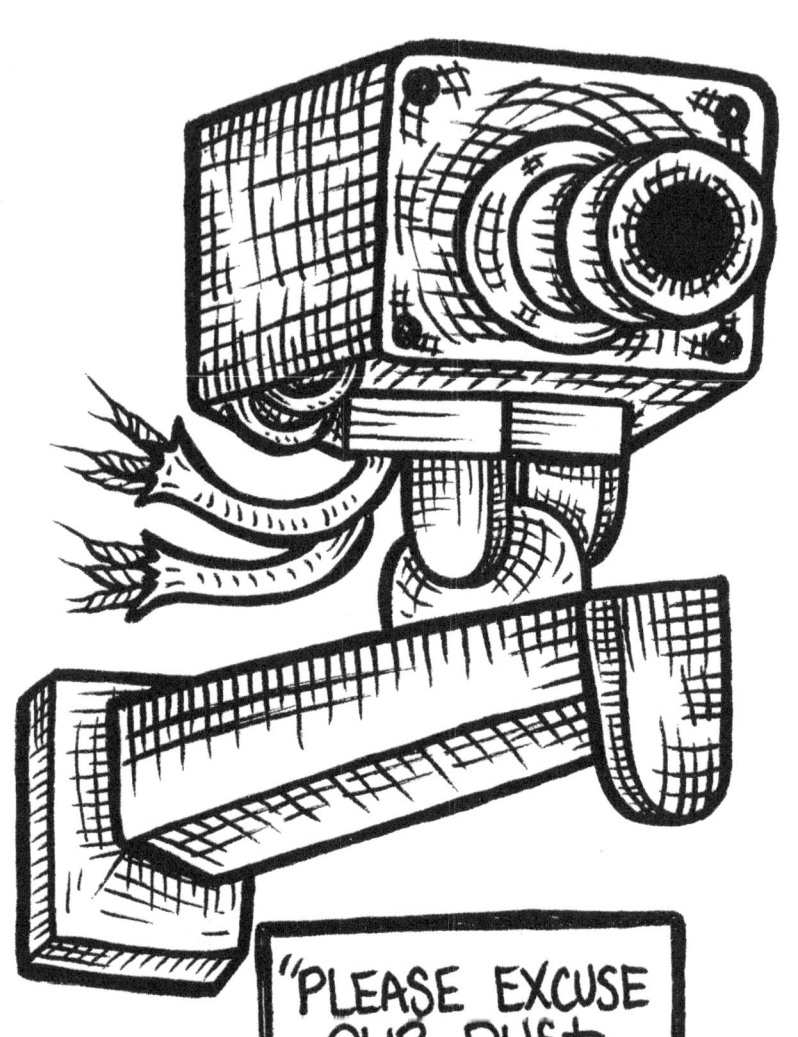

"TWO WEIRD-LOOKING NEW YORKERS
ABDUCTING THE WELCOME MAT
TO THE HIPPIE CAPITAL OF THE EASTERN
UNITED STATES"

WHAT WOULD CHARLES INGALLS DO?

The less sense everything else makes, the more sense that question makes. To me, anyway.

When I take my blinders off and look at where and how we're living, confusion and disillusionment are never far behind. There is a strange falseness to so much of it, but also a head-shaking amount of reality, and I'm not sure which is more disconcerting.

As I walked out the door of my apartment building today *(it opens on to a relatively passive street and is directly between an antique store and a fancy hair salon)* a guy spouted off *"Watch where you're going, motherfucker!"* In his defense, I think he was partially kidding- though in bad taste- and also trying to impress his friend. It was dark out, and my luck being what it is, I firmly responded with *"Watch your mouth. Let's start over... "* and he immediately apologized and continued on his way.

The problem isn't that he said it to *me*- the problem is that he said it at all. Opening that door could have been my neighbor's parents leaving after having dinner together in his apartment, it could have been my landlord *(old and capable, but certain to be upset by that)*, or it could have been someone that had just moved to the city, and being addressed in that manner may have really thrown them off.

Hearing a seemingly non-confrontational, preppily-dressed idiot fire volatile profanity at a stranger that he had not yet even seen was just another sad example of how far the little house has traveled from the prairie. Everyone finds their amusement in slightly different ways, but there are some birds that just shouldn't be allowed to fly.

If by himself, I believe Charles Ingalls probably would have responded much like I did. If his wife or daughters were with him, or he witnessed the instance-in-question happen to one of the hypotheticals listed above, I imagine *(enjoyably)* that there would have been a simple yet thorough thrashing- both in the interest of defending honor and teaching a lesson.

In my opinion, that is right. You reap what you sow- or, at least you did when the world was still real. The de-evolution of personal accountability should not absolve one of repercussion for inappropriate actions. Charles Ingalls knew better 100+ years ago; I think often of the simple and timeless concepts that have been nearly abandoned, and how different the current world landscape would look if they were still even partially in play.

If Charles Ingalls owed someone something, or made a commitment to a project, he honored it- even if it meant being inconvenienced or putting himself in a sometimes far less-than-ideal situation. Injury, near starvation, sleeplessness, loneliness, physical hardship, compromise of convenience and comfort... Honoring responsibility always stood far taller than avoiding inconvenience. That, too, is right.

The few times in my life that I have gone against that notion are by far and away my most regretful. The part of you that entered into the commitment or took on the debt *(financial, emotional or otherwise)* should not be disrespected by the current, misguided version of you attempting to flee; Personal safety and self-preservation considered, of course.

If he crossed paths with someone that was down, Charles Ingalls helped them up- even if he may not have particularly liked them or even known them. And if someone he cared for was down, all the stops were pulled out to right the ship- personal convenience and comfort aside.

None of that is antiquated, 19th-century nonsense or idealistic zealotry; Just a semi-lost set of values that served many good people well for hundreds of years. Charles Ingalls was simply an easily-accessible example that resonated with me and made an impact.

The convoluted path of our progressive, modern world has undermined age-old tenets responsible for setting a bar so high that it has now been able to fall this low and still be seen as acceptable.

Our forefathers deserve both a pat on the back, and a cover for their eyes.

SHE'LL NEVER KNOW...

———

Quickly and quietly, the trapdoor had closed on me. My attempts to reflect on things I had enjoyed or loved were immediately darkened by vicious pain and uncustomary confusion. They would not relent, and it felt like there was no escape.

In the span of a few short months I moved back to my hometown after a nearly 10-year absence, watched a successful business we had built collapse in on itself, and in the turmoil allowed a lifetime of unmanaged mental health issues get way ahead of me. I pushed away a person that would have loved and cared for me forever, lost the house I misguidedly bought upon my return, and left my brother unemployed during the Christmas season.

For much of that time I was struggling with an injury that left me sleeping sitting up with near-constant pain in my back and legs. The surgery performed to repair it did not do its job, and after the pain and recovery of *that* process, the original pain had barely changed.

Now I was simply weaker, but no less uncomfortable, and avoiding at all costs becoming drug-reliant to cope with it. All the while I was in the midst of losing my mind, and was somehow good enough at it that none of the right people were asking any of the right questions.

It wasn't that I felt I had nothing further to offer. I was just so profoundly disappointed with myself that my already challenged self-esteem and self-worth had no chance of making any sort of credible stand. Our main business had failed, I exiled the one person that may have been able to offer the clarity and stability I needed, I was in constant, serious, physical pain, and each of those failures was impacting those that I cared about in negative ways.

I have never paid much mind to how things impact me, but I over-care about how even small things impact others; In this particular period of time, that flawed strategy got way out ahead of me.

Day-to-day I was functioning mostly on instinct. I had begun to learn how to talk myself out of pain- if even for just brief periods of time- in efforts to not simply take the pills and try to forget. If I stayed positive-minded and distracted, I could make it; I truly thought I was making it.

I had developed a small training business, and it was something that even back in 2009 I had already put many years of work into. It provided structure, and the people that *(much to my daily surprise)* kept showing up provided motivation. When I was engaged in either my or their process of learning, the seas were somewhat calm. The danger zones were weekends and nighttime... I would sit with the cat, and think, and try to write, and watch things I had seen before simply to feel any sort of familiarity and comfort when I was feeling none in any other aspect or moment of my life.

When I moved correctly and deliberately, the pain was manageable; If I made a drastic mistake, such as leaning down too quickly to tie my shoes, or redirecting my movement without first stabilizing myself, it became anything but. I would black out occasionally simply from moving in a slightly compromised position; Sometimes the pain and tension would just turn the lights out.

All of it gave me some very real perspective on the relativity of discomfort, on my own capacity for physical endurance, and a possibly unsafe dose of humility for someone that had spent most of his life developing physical skillsets that appeared to be disappearing before his eyes.

I felt no lifeline, and saw no endgame.

Unless you have done something so morally detestable that you deserve to feel pain by your own hand and leave this earth in shame, there is always a better path out of the dark. Reading this is not likely to be helpful to those in the midst of, because once your brain malfunctions to that degree, very little sense can be made of very much... and you are never nearly as in control of any of it as you think you are. I thought I had it... managed... But that ended up being the furthest thing from the truth.

There is a nearly-infinite stream of opinions and notions and debate about the how's and why's of such things. My simple take on it is this: Each of our brains has the power to trick us; Some simply capitalize more maliciously on the ability.

When the die is cast, you no longer see a choice in the matter. It isn't weakness, or strength, or success, or failure that governs the game, its chemicals. When I woke up that morning, I had no idea that nine hours later I would take enough pills to kill me, on purpose, and calmly standing in my kitchen. But that is exactly what happened.

It all just made sense, and yet none of it made sense. Everything was neutral, but just so heavy that it didn't even allow me the panic and dread and redirection I should have been feeling.

In the past two decades I've been prescribed every brain drug and ham-fistedly diagnosed with every mental ailment that the blue pad has boxes for. Even after listening to my reasonable, intelligent analysis and description of why I sometimes struggle mentally, the first response was always assign a scary diagnosis and drug it into submission. I would often start the drugs, become unsettled with either what they really did or what I anticipated them doing, and then stop. That was very likely not the best strategy, but I would then and now rather be a product of myself than a product of their product.

I was thinking, but it wasn't working. All I wanted was quiet. I found the cat, told her everything would be OK, ate an impolite handful of narcotic pain medicine and high-dose brain medicine, and sat down on the ground. Even then, I wasn't worried about myself. Through the fuzz and fury and frustration, and soon confusion, and relief, and elation, I remember thinking about the fact that my parents and brother would likely have to move all my stuff, and what a hassle that would be. And, who would care for the cat. At that point the system was completely broken, and was about to shut down.

I don't know how long I was out, or why I woke up at all. As I lay on the kitchen floor barely able to see, the cat climbed on my chest as she often does, and head-butted me in the chin, as she often does. I don't know exactly what did what, or why, or how, *(and would be lying for the sake of continuity if I pretended to)* but an emotion stirred in me as she sat there, and the panic I should have felt earlier finally appeared.

I could barely feel anything. It was as if I were crawling on clouds, or bubbles, or pudding. I was disoriented beyond belief, and began opening low cabinets because I was unable to stand. I found and gulped from a clear bottle *(which ended up being vinegar),* and threw up many of the pills.

I don't know how long I was out, again, but this time I at least woke up knowing I had woken up. Everything was still the furthest from right, but I was awake, and there was at least enough clarity to be grateful for that fact.

I must have been absent for long enough to inspire worry, because after waking up for the third time, I heard my parents enter through the garage. Things were clearly not right, and I was taken to the hospital.

I only gave part of the story; Thankfully that was enough to let me recover and exit in somewhat short-order, though not without some contention. There was still an air of denial on my part, and it made me indignant and uncooperative towards the idea of staying any longer than I already had, though it almost certainly would have been valuable.

I have thought about that day, every day; How it could have gone, and nearly went. How it ended up where it did; How *I* ended up where *I* did. Why my usual rational, logical, calculating mind couldn't see the forest for the trees, and why something that made no sense made so much sense. And, mostly, I think of how improbable it was that the very thing I oddly thought of last was the same one that rattled my fuckin' cage at the very right time... and that she'll never even know.

Her simple, familiar gesture was the only reason-I believe- that everything didn't end right there.

—

It took me six years to finish writing this. I began in 2010, and decided soon after that I didn't want to complete or publish it. I had revisited it since and kept the same perspective, but in light of several recent events and out of a desire to close an open door, it is now fucking done.

Again: Unless you have done something so morally detestable that you deserve to feel pain by your own hand and leave this earth in shame, there is always a better path out of the dark.

Reading this is not likely to be helpful to those in the midst of, because once your brain malfunctions to that degree, very little sense can be made of very much... and you are never nearly as in control of any of it as you think you are.

I thought I had it... managed. But that ended up being the furthest thing from the truth.

I couldn't save myself from myself; No matter what I accomplish or what may happen from here out, knowing that it really all came down to luck and timing beyond my control provides an unrelenting humility and clarity, and a sharp, tight tether to reality.

THOUGHT CRIME

What is *"Thought Crime"*?

"A thoughtcrime is an occurrence or instance of controversial or socially unacceptable thoughts."

The term comes from the novel *'1984'* by **George Orwell**. 1984 is the story of a man, and a society, that eroded into a cycle of forced control, blind routine and ultimately a total loss of free will. Out of fear, the citizens fight their natural instincts to think and act freely, and, also out of fear, the rulers of the society fight to suppress them.

No one on either side conceptualized or realized any sort of progressive or suitable destiny; Their lives began and ended a series of pre-manufactured actions and pre-determined conclusions...

Just like many in our world now: In full possession of their own free will, yet not self-possessed enough to follow where it leads.

As it applies today, in our perception: Much of society has devolved to a state of near-mindlessness. Between the instant access, constant contact, and faceless unaccountability of our digital and pre-programmed lives, autonomy and independence are replaced too often and too easily by convenience and thoughtless pattern.

Our interpretation of *"Thought crime"* is simply a counterpoint to herd mentality, and a call to arms towards reaching true potential by never being led blindly; Assert will over your mind, and turn your strongest thoughts into even stronger actions.

Dissent and questioning lead to confidence and evolution, while complacency leads to loss of clarity.

Think, act, and become a stronger, more independent version of yourself than our modern society wants you to be;

Thought crime does not equal death, as the villains in *'1984' (and the dominant influences in our society)* would lead you to believe.

Life

devoid of vivid and voracious,

sometimes seditious,

dangerous

turns of the mind

is no life at all.

THE CURSE OF AWARENESS, PART TWO

There is a gloom that lives here when the weather turns mean, and people either fight it like an enemy, or succumb to it, and spend an entire season in misery. I've never really minded it, with the exception of watching how it makes others treat, *others*.

The drive back to home base was short; A small consolation for the cargo I was retrieving being heavy, clunky, dirty, and freezing fucking cold. Metal pipes, even stored inside a garage door, didn't seem to warm much past the single-digit temperature outside it. I drove appropriately cautiously, considering both the unusual weather and my irregular passengers.

Driving towards an underpass, I noticed a commotion.

Cars were honking and swerving, in very tight quarters, and for a reason I couldn't quite distinguish until I got closer. Upon under-passing, I saw the obstruction:

It was a man. In a wheelchair. That had tipped over.

Leaning precariously on a small curb in the center of the bridge, clearly immobile, was a man in a wheelchair. That had tipped over.

I got the feeling that good people get when they see an animal dart into the road, or a person unknowingly moving towards danger; The feeling that no one likes, but that has saved many lives, and that sends the appropriate senses into immediate overdrive.

I also got the feeling that bad people get when they see worse people acting like the *worst* people; The feeling that no one likes, that has taken many lives, and that sends the inappropriate senses into immediate overdrive.

I put my flashers on, hustled to upright the man *(amidst the blare of horns)*, and did so accompanied by a panic and anger that I have felt many times before, and that each time I hope to never feel again.

The man squeezed my arm as he uttered a thank you, and it struck me like an unseen blow to the back. I don't know why, exactly, but the oddity of the situation coupled with the cold reality of people's non-reaction crushed me. I felt the palpable soul-sink that occurs in an unpleasant instant, but that will last as long as its inciting incident goes unreconciled.

I am positive he had tipped over before, and he made his way quickly once righted, but none of that changed the fact that he was left lying on his side, in traffic, under a fucking bridge, while people swerved around him and honked at the inconvenience.

Where. The fuck. Am I?

Nothing made me feel good about my actions, and everything made me want to smash windshields and extract the sardines.

Had I not made a semi-career out of resisting the urge to permanently injure those that mistreat others, I would have removed one of the large metal tools I was transporting and began giving the soulless bodies sneaking by something to actually honk at.

But.

That's not how the world turns.

Yet.

THE CURSE OF AWARENESS,
PART THREE

If I wasn't looking, I wouldn't have seen; I'm never really sure if that is better or worse.

Any attentive, creative mind could write volumes *(and I imagine even semi-interesting ones)* about the oddity and unpredictability of the American grocery store. I can't recall a trip in which I didn't see something that, even on my widely-sliding scale, wouldn't be considered major-league odd.

How we perceive what we see is what keeps the innocuous from becoming monotonous, I guess.

I've been forcing myself to stay even busier than usual lately; An often-unsuccessful attempt at a distraction from myself. I didn't need anything, but wanted ice cream, and went to the smaller of the local grocery stores to get it. Independently owned, single location, and a strange mix of *normal* things and fancy things. I imagine the hybridization is a necessity, since if someone is spending $8 on a bag of hand-made, organic, ethically-sourced supercookies, they may need to save a bit on name-brand white rice and toothpaste.

The outing was a non-necessity, and I was in no particular hurry. I noticed an interesting young couple pull in a few spaces down in a well-kept older convertible, and waited a few moments to exit the car and move behind them, as opposed to walking near arm-in-arm in the small lot. They would very likely never have noticed; I would have noticed.

In a world in which the list seems to get shorter every day, it was nice to observe what seemed to be two kind, pleasant people interacting with each other and the world around them like non-assholes; Disappointed but not surprised that such a thing, is such a surprise.

I got my ice cream, had a short and pleasant interaction with a woman that has been working there each and every time I have visited *(and always remembers me)*, and made my way. As I walked back into the parking lot I noticed another boy + girl couple.

I'm not a big fan of glaring generalities; For lack of interest in detailedly describing someone so uninteresting, let's say the boy was a... metal hipster. His physical and superficial aesthetic did not match: Fat and physically unkempt, with an attempt at a sharp outfit, and a girl by his side that must have been either blind or indentured. Or, band; I always forget what misguided enchantment playing even terrible music can be.

As they walked, he moved away from her, and towards the older convertible. It became clear quite quickly that he was not admiring the bodywork, and *was* actually snooping to see if there was anything not tied-down that he could walk with. I gave it another few seconds, in the interest of fairness, and then addressed him.

"Hey man, is that your car?" He turned and responded quickly *"Yeah. It's my car. Why?"* ... *"Well, it's not your fucking car, since I just watched people that aren't you get out of it five minutes ago, so get away from it."* Clearly not versed in the school of confrontational strategy, or listening, or not being a total fucking moron, he replied *"Mind your own business, and it IS my car."*

I am saintly patient, right up until... I'm not. *"Get the fuck away from that car, and walk on. I'm going to stand here until you do, so fucking get moving."* And... as if out of an *"Idiots that wander into my life"* playbook, he says *"Is there something you'd like to do about it, bro?"*

When I document situations like this I will occasionally describe my outfit, or another piece of circumstance that makes a response I received particularly curious to me. Today, I was coming from the gym, it was abnormally hot, I was wearing a tank top with rough-looking symbols printed on it, and relatively small shorts. There is, in my opinion, no way that I looked like easy prey right at that moment.

I did not want to fight, and was even surer that he didn't, so I responded as if I absolutely did, and *"Bro'ed"* right back at him. *"Well motherfucker, I will put you to sleep and take your girlfriend, if that's the route you want to go..."* Walking towards him while asserting myself elicited the desired response *"I wasn't trying to start anything, for real man. I'm going. Chill out."*

Other least-favorite things: When the very fucking person that heightens a situation tells the hive they poked to calm down.

(Some local punk rock wrestling nerd started a fight with us a while back, and as I was choking him, he was tapping me. Same thing. *YOU started trouble. We are not friends, and we are not training. Don't tell me to chill out, and, don't attempt to tap in a streetfight, especially one you started...)*

As threatened, I watched until they had cleared the lot. She was clearly mortified, and I was sympathetic. I would have a hard time believing things were the same for them, even right as they left the lot. That is, unless society has truly shrunken to a state in which petty thievery, cowardice, lack of accountability, and disrespect are so common that it is no less than what *"she"* expects.

Less, unfortunately, is what we have been made to expect.

As expectations continue to fall, I appreciate so profoundly those that rise past them, and become more vigilant by the day in attempting to exceed my own.

LESSONS OF LOSS

When I was a kid, there were still *(and only)* home-phones. I'm not old, but I'm old enough to have had the good fortune to experience many now-dead things that required deliberateness and patience... though we didn't know or appreciate that at the time.

The simple act of hand-dialing a number, the tolerance of... a busy signal. The fact that if you missed a call, you may not know until either someone told you, or they called back. Clear to see why optimal communication required evolution, but valuable to recall some of the virtues the inefficiency helped develop.

Sometimes, though, one edge of the knife is sharper and more malicious than the other... As is the case with the most important phone call I have ever missed.

I was goofing around with the neighbors; Stirring up dust, breaking something so we could figure out how to fix it, or building something so we could figure out how to break it. It was past dusk on a warm spring night, and time to go home.

I had missed a call. The handwritten recap said *"Chris: 8:40pm, no message"*. Then, it was not thought of twice to return a call the next day, unless a specific directive was given otherwise. And just after 9pm... The time had not yet come when a phone call for any reason at any hour was common fare. In school the next day we were sure to catch up on anything he wanted to tell me on the phone.

Such was the world, before it became a technological macrocosm of careless instantaneousness and largely unnecessary immediacy.

Chris was absent from school the next day. Odd, but not alarming... Until, it was.

As it occurred in a pre-device-based-Newspeak world, true voice-based interaction began to circulate that something had happened to Chris. Although I have notes from the time surrounding these events, all they said about this day was *"No one knew the truth yet"*, followed by *"Heard from Meghan. Chris is dead."*

The girl that shared the news with me was not someone that would have moved in my orbit, ordinarily; Chris and I were quite close, and she knew that. She was also a friend of his, and as it did with all of us, shock and grief blurred any notion of adolescent caste system or social-order hierarchy.

As depicted in any movie on-or-relating-to the topic, small groups huddled together in stairways, girls walked arm-in-arm, crying down the hallways... Boys looked solemn, but tried not to look *"weak"*.

Details were surfacing, but the blur still outweighed the clear. We learned at the very end of the day that Chris had hanged himself in his bedroom the night before. I learned the next day that he had not died immediately, but that his parents had found him, taken him to the hospital, and then lost him. Once examined and investigated, it appeared to have been more a plea for attention than an actual attempt, and that it had simply *(and not simply)* gone as wrong as any cry for help could have.

In the same distasteful manner as followed several other situations I stumbled into as a youth and young adult, I was a different person after that day, and not in a good way.

Chris was the charismatic ladies' man, with the gorgeous older sister and the cool car. His car was the first place I ever heard Black Sabbath, and his stories were the first I heard of... a lot of things. This was my also first look into the vicious unpredictability of the human mind, as-on paper- what happened made no sense to anyone that had ever met him; Especially the friend he had called on the phone, not long before it occurred.

I attended the wake, and at that time, had not yet

been exposed to such sadness and widespread grief. I had been to funerals for people I knew and cared for, but a kid, taken in that way... In a community where such a thing was, at the very least, uncommon...

It was nearly debilitating, and combined with the fact that many in attendance were no more than casual school acquaintances and wouldn't have had anything to do with me outside of these heightened circumstances, it felt even more isolating and volatile. Since isolation and volatility were already concepts I had made unintentional friends with, I chose not to attend the funeral.

Though I've lost many friends since, and far too many in far too similar a manner, I have not attended another funeral. I pay respects in my way; I attempt to pay respect with my entire life. I know the weight and gravity such things hold over me, and also how easily they can all join together and drag me under.

The fact that we had been made to endure a loss such as this together manufactured a fleeting sense of class camaraderie in the weeks following, however all pieces of the situation drove me to feel otherwise. Certainly a bad habit that I've held on to since, but circumstantial unity was never a notion that stuck with me; I isolated and removed myself even more from "conventional" life, and the paths it set me on and doors opened by doing so are certainly the only un-scarring take-aways from such a sad and overwhelming event.

I liken the psychological aftermath of such a thing to the storied BB lodged in the knuckle; Everything still mostly functional, but routinely painful, and truly unforgettable.

All aspects of what transpired were sharp and mean in ways I was unprepared for, and also as confusing and troublesome as they were avoidable; By me (maybe).

We'll never know. But rest assured, I'll always wonder.

TIME UNDER TENSION[1]

I over-think. But I am not the oft-seen *"over-thinker/ under-doer".*

I think hard about deep water because I know I can and will put myself in it, and that it often gets deeper far quicker than even my over-thinkery could account for. *Anticipatory pre-redundancy system*; If you're thinking about a single back-up plan, then the need for two is probably already one step ahead of you.

I did not over-think the booking of a recent trip to Salt Lake City to talk and train with a bunch of people I had never met in an environment I had never been in with a purpose that was completely *(intriguingly)* murky. When the offer was made, I immediately signed on the dotted line and began my plan. My lack of hesitation speaks loudly to the offerers' quality and quietly to my mental disclarity.

[1] Originally seen in Raze magazine, Issue #1, 2018.

My *"plan"* was to figure out at all costs how to unravel the tightening knot that my body and brain had found themselves in prior to making a daunting cross-country trip to talk physicality and philosophy with people so interesting to me that I would have walked the distance had that been the directive.

I had a spinal fusion surgery in 2012 after a less-invasive version went poorly in 2009. The invasion in 2012 also went poorly, and it impacted my left big toe and leg irreparably. I was informed of a 15% chance of return to normal function; I don't want to know their percentage had the mistake they made been figured in. They tried to fix what they broke with too much medicine, for too long, and with too little care. It did damage, helped very little, and it was all I could do to stay ahead of it. Until, I couldn't.

Based on a previous haphazard removal of a prescription steroid, this next exit was handled with care, but still proved far less than cooperative. *(Because this is boring, and ultimately just the perimeter of the point)* I will say that the steroid removal presented an element of physical and psychological dysfunction that I would not wish on any but three of my worst enemies; Nothing worked, yet I made it work, because it had to work. Until, it wouldn't.

I knew I had a few months to right the ship, and did not doubt for one minute *(until the week before I was to leave)* that I would do so. It was very important to me to be at my best. People do not offer me things; I am the proverbial squeaky wheel- We are where we are because we made it so *(for better or worse)...* Here were a group of people that I respected extending a thorns-removed olive branch, and there was not a moment of doubt *(until the week before the trip)* as to whether I would grab hold.

The primary inviter had some idea of the situation I was in, but only because I wanted to pre-qualify that I was not usually a tipsy, clumsy, poorly-coordinated mess, assuming I did make it out at all.

I was eating Borax *(cleaning product)* as a hail-Mary fix-it strategy, bracing for a 3/1000 prior to putting on or taking off my shoes because I was prone to falling down, and using any manner of trick, trap, and anchor to keep training the main movement patterns; There was no sense in getting weaker while I was getting weaker.

The removal of the steroid had baited some sort of inflammatory arthritis, and the drug had been falsely supporting my adrenals for so long that without it, they no longer felt any obligation to support me. I could barely walk, think, or sleep. But I trained every day. Some days I fell over, and each day I did not fucking care.

Someone I respected offered me something I appreciated, and I was going to do it justice if it fucking killed me; Maybe it's a character flaw.

A week before the trip, the near-comical reality of what was going on set in during a moment of decaffeinated weakness, and I nearly pulled the plug. I was torn as to whether it was more disrespectful to accept an offer to be among high-level life participants such as these in the state I was in, or to respectfully withdraw and not risk the humiliation, pain, and emasculation that a trip in my current state would certainly create.

I taped my wrists *(the only way I could close my hands at that time)*, thought about some hard things I had done and seen, put on music made by people that had done and seen much harder, and pushed myself as far and hard as I could. Even in its respectively pathetic measure, the work provided the moment of clarity I needed to decide that suffering will always be better than settling, for me, and that no matter what happened before, during, or after, it was all more appealing than being left to wonder.

I fell down in the airport, twice, and took 30-minute cold showers at the end of each day in an attempt to even get my body to operate as a system. I used my entire non-existent 401K in Tiger Balm in two-and-a-half days, and my hands shook so bad when I wasn't shaking hands that I was sure anyone present believed me to be nervous, or a junkie; Not sure which would have been worse.

We talked, we trained, and until reading this I had hoped most had no idea that anything odd was even afoot; Their motivation and camaraderie *(and insubordination and sincerity)*, elicited highest clarity, in the midst of some hearty adversity.

The psychological transcends with a comma... It is only the purely physical that ends with a period; I was making the mistake of perceiving this as a task of body, when in fact it was just another devilish motherfucking mind game.

All told, all parts, were well-worth playing.

THE LAST RUNG ON THE LADDER

———

Everyone's gut talks to them differently; I'm still not sure whether the way mine communicates is a blessing or a curse.

I moved to California in January of 1999 to work at what could be considered the only *"real"* job I've ever had. I've never *not* worked- I started when I was 15 and haven't stopped since- but it has always been for either small companies, for myself, or in a placeholder-type position while I was occupied *(or about to be...)* with travel for bike riding or music.

Moving to the LA area from my hometown of Rochester, New York for a real job was a decision I did not take lightly, and once made I had no intention of putting in a simply mediocre run at it. As soon as the amazing opportunity presented itself I took it, and the heartache of leaving my family, friends, and hometown was matched and possibly even overshadowed by the clarity I felt towards the potential magnitude of the situation I was entering. Working for a major bike company (among some of my childhood heroes) was something I never could have imagined would lead me into the murky and dysfunctional situations I would later come upon.

Existing in the action sports industry in Southern California afforded me more than a fair share of interaction with people I could neither relate to nor take seriously, and when I saw yet another trimmed, skinny goatee climb out of a giant, lifted Ford truck at a skatepark in Orange County, I had profiled and dismissed it before the boot had even hit the pavement.

Over walked a tall, good-looking, dark-haired guy wearing a button-up shirt with a big fly collar, oversized pants, and dress shoes... wheeling what appeared to be a really nice BMX bike. Unless he had a change of clothes in one of the gigantic pizza-pockets on the back of his jeans, it looked as though he were going to ride the skatepark in an outfit that would have been more fitting at a Top-40 nightclub in West Hollywood. In an industry and region of the country where people were routinely made fun of for simply having the seat of their bike too high, the oddity of his outfit made it a spectacle, and a curious distraction.

Once the ice was cracked during routine exposure and casual conversation over the coming months, it became clear that Andy was the troubled, caring kind- much like most of the people I've been closest to in my life- and also extremely insecure, but for no discernable reason. Another addition to the unfortunate and bewildering script: Handsome, extremely talented in a variety of useful ways, and a do-anything-for-you sort. Plane re-routed and new arrival airport is two hours from the intended? Andy will get you, and somehow make the headache into an amusing adventure.

Having a fondness develop for someone you assumed you were going to dislike always seems to add extra depth or deepened authenticity to whatever shape the relationship took from that point, since it was forced to rise from adversity.

He ended up taking a sales position at the same company I was in, and he was preternaturally good at it. His bad habits followed him, and over the next few years, everyone in our circle did everything they could to chase him back to the things he loved and excelled at each time his demons tried to drag him away.

Never discourteous, never disheveled, never so focused on himself that he couldn't be asked to lend a hand to others; It was his casual day-to-day demeanor and admirable code of conduct that kept anyone from noticing that he was drowning.

He had moved into a room in the beautiful home of a friend and co-worker of ours, and the hope was that the proximity to normalcy would help him out of the dark, but it did not appear to be working. After receiving a frantic call, I hurried over to the house and found Andy in his room, with a loaded gun to his throat.

I believe strongly that the pure discourtesy of me being forced to intervene was the deterrent he needed that day, coupled with not wanting to disappoint someone that had put faith, time, and effort into him in both personal and professional realms. I was not afraid for my safety while intervening, as no matter how convoluted his mind was I knew he would never harm me, but I was enormously fearful of mishandling something so volatile.

It took several significant missteps and some pretty flagrant irresponsibility for the owners of the company to intervene, though when they finally did, I was tasked with delivering the news. I told them he was really struggling, had a lot of support within the company, and really needed the stability the job provided, but *"risk"* vs. *"reward"* for careless people that only see black, white, and green looked a lot different than it did to me; No professional risk could be outweighed by the potential of personal reward.

I was ordered to fire Andy, on a Friday afternoon, as per the handbook. Another co-worker was made to be in attendance as well, but I said the words, and knew it to be a mistake in both fact and conscience before I had even begun the wrong-minded task. The twists and pitfalls and gravity of what was unfolding within the company, and the amount of daunting-but- positive things I was spearheading, infused pressure to tow the company line even though I knew in heart and head that it was wrong. If I had flat-out refused,

I believe many of the valuable projects we had in the works would have suffered; That presents as nothing more than trite, weak-minded justification, now with all things considered.

I fired Andy, and he killed himself the next day.

If humanity's blight of selfishness that I had stood against and written about throughout my entire young adult life and avoided in all aspects of my *"career"* could manifest in such a profound way by my hand, there was a chance *(at least in my mind)* that I had been mistaken about the strength of my conviction to a self-less path. In a time when the questioning I was doing of myself was already nothing short of debilitating, adding that level of self-doubt to the list taught me some lessons in darkness that I definitely did not need to learn.

The end result is the end result. Of course there is rational discussion and point/ counterpoint conversation that could be had, but they would all end with the commiserators eyes on the ground, shoulders lazily shrugged, while the simple truth remains:

Were there other serious factors in play? *Yes.*

Had they all performed their uprising and been put back down, time and time again, with Andy's life impacted but intact? *Yes.*

Did I cut the final fray of tightrope that resulted in the loss of that life?

Yes.

Was it possibly just a slight tipping of the already-in-motion *"Hand of Fate"*, and not an unexpected shove off of a seemingly stable ledge?

Anything is possible.

It is a possibility that he had planned it all along, and regardless of how his week went, Saturday night he was going to make damn sure of how the next one started.

But.

Hypothesis does not ease guilt or sorrow, and compartmentalizing the negative *(especially that which we carry a burden of fault for)* into the *"Everything happens for a reason"* folder, doesn't either. There is no new-agey phrasing that can distract from the fact that I fired a good friend against my better judgment, while they were struggling, and he took his own life the next day. I will read that sentence until the day I die and never feel even 1% better about it than I do right now.

I've made a self-preservation-measure of peace with my mistake, but that doesn't mean it will ever sit still, or play nice; As it shouldn't.

Close friends, appreciated acquaintances from underground culture, people I looked up to for many of the same madnesses and idiosyncrasies that led them down their path to self-destruction...

The self-guided hand of doom has not discriminated in my life, and instead of the impact of the blows softening *(as many tend to do with time)*, it now all just seems more horrible, and somehow, avoidable.

Several such situations have affected me in ways I still feel every day, but even the heavy ones can't hold a candle to the heartbreak and self-scrutiny that resulted from the loss of my friend Andy.

HATE, BLOOD, PAIN, PRAYING, AND WAITING[1]

———

I wish the world were different,
But this is what we've got.

I wish the times weren't signing,
But minding me, they're not.

I wish that hate was useful,
I've got far more than I need

I wish that lessons learned themselves,
but until they do, we bleed.

———

[1] Lines and passages, 2011-2018.

Blood can pour from the soul in the same way it can from the skin.

Working to avoid spilling it is misguided self-limitation, and just as futile as attempting to avoid the burning of true exertion;

When it comes, it comes.

When it happens, it happens.

Skin heals, and souls strengthen,

and neither are given the chance to do so

without first being cut open.

There is a truth to pain that few other things in the world can tell;

The self-realization it inflicts in beginning, the humility and gratitude it grants at the end.

Real pain is both truth serum and intoxicant;

Both poison and antidote.

It shows the best of the good, and the worst of the evil.

Sometimes it covers you like a blanket, sometimes it pours like water.

Sometimes it burns, like fire.

In its hex you feel most human,

under its lure you feel clear and sharp,

and now it is yours.

You prayed for a station in life that never came,

you had eyes on a prize that mere *'want'* could not claim.

You are the epitome of mediocrity,

and your *'now'* is your destiny.

You'll plod through what's left,

never moving the needle,

and you'll gripe the whole time...

Too dark to be good,

too light to be evil.

Our suffering

is the slow-cracking chrysalis

of personal evolution;

We cannot rush the escape,

or we risk emerging

incomplete.

+

We must bear down,

breathe patiently through the fog and grime,

and wait for our time.

ABOUT THE AUTHOR

Long before the large-scale homogenization and widespread acceptance of underground cultures into the mainstream, Greg Walsh followed the unlit path, weathered the storms it presented, and embraced the outcastism that set the tone for all that followed in his life.

Resourcefulness was hard-learned, any advancement was hard-earned, and each and every step was both daunting and vitally important.

Describing his relationship with BMX and hardcore music as a *"love affair"* would be an understatement. Each was its own vicious and driving force, and no stone was left unturned in the pursuit of progress in either.

The fuse lit by the early influences in Greg's life continued to burn even when all else was dark; Strength in solitude and clarity in defiance were to be the most valuable lessons any culture or character could teach him, even as steep as the learning curve often was.

Rounded out both physically and mentally with martial arts and strength training at the turn of the millennium, Greg is the proverbial eternal youth, and proof that even as much as some things change, the most important stay the same.

Advancements, missteps, successes, and failures- each born of disordered intellect and an unquenchable obsession to search- have been collected and documented as reminiscence, entertainment, catharsis, and cautionary tale.

Suffer, endure, think, act, subvert, provoke... And take good notes while doing so.

THE MEPHISTO GROUP

Made in the USA
Middletown, DE
17 April 2022

64185269R00119